DON'T CHASE YOUR

DREAMS

CATCH THEM

I0225148

By Author:

Sean Alexander Hamilton

Don't Chase Your Dreams Catch Them

First Published in 2012

Second Printing in 2020 Revised and Updated Version

Published by AlexanderHamiltonsInsights

Printed in America

www.alexanderhamltonsinsights.com

Book Cover Designer:

Olga Vynnychenko

*DON'T CHASE YOUR
DREAMS CATCH THEM*

Table of Contents

*DON'T CHASE YOUR
DREAMS CATCH THEM*

DEDICATED: TO ALL THE

DREAMERS OUT THERE!!!

*DON'T CHASE YOUR
DREAMS CATCH THEM*

INTRODUCTION

Now I have always wondered about people and their dreams. I would wonder how many of us as had a dream, but it was never fully realized? Well if you are reading this book then it is time to realize that dream and make it happen for you. So many people go on in life and chase, chase, chase, chase, and chase what they're after and never reach it.

It is due to the simple fact, if you keep running and chasing after the ball (dream); then you will simply run into the wall. Well there goes the ball out of range from your glove and no matter how much you jump you will be doing nothing but just that; jumping in thin air.

For I know that because it is just what I was doing. I was jumping in thin air with runaway thoughts and doing my best to chase those thoughts. Now in this book I will explain what this will do to you in a chapter title exactly that Runaway Thoughts.

You see I had all of these runaway thoughts within my mind and I was getting nowhere. Until I came out with my first book entitled Defeating Financial Anger in September 29, 2010. I had finally reached and caught my dream and became a published author.

So I told myself if I could catch my dream then why couldn't other people catch there's? Before that had happen, my younger bother reached his and came out with his first CD Tracked called What Are You Waiting For E.P....... His band's name is entitled Marvlec! In that one song (what are you waiting for!!!!) He touch's on this principle of what this book is based on of catching your dreams instead of chasing them. So if you can't get the context of this writing then go to Youtube and search for

DON'T CHASE YOUR
DREAMS CATCH THEM

his song what are you waiting for under Marvlec. Then listen to that song and you will have clearer understanding of the context of this book.

So with that as you go through the pages of this very powerful book you will be able to be all you could be. I will walk you through just how to catch that dream of yours. But in order to do this you will have to chase that dream through these pages first.

Then finally at exactly the right moment you will be able to stop the chase and become the catcher that I know you all are!

Sean Alexander Hamilton

*DON'T CHASE YOUR
DREAMS CATCH THEM*

CHAPTER ONE

IDENTIFY YOUR DREAM

"Dreams are just dreams. We all have them. Until we understand and accept the adversity that comes with it, we will never be able to make it a reality, a goal to unravel. Accept the adversity… and allow the impossible to become possible."

Sasha Gomez

Throughout your life you will have many goals (a.k.a.) DREAMS. Your vision of your dreams will change often throughout this journey called life. Now when doing your best

to have a clear mental vision of these goals
there will be changes to that dream! Exactly
how many you will have will be up to the clear
mental vision that you carry with you. This will
be the most challenging test you will go
through, when catching your dream.

This is when the actual hunt or chase begins
for that dream. It could last for years, months,
or days and in most cases it will last for years.
Until you have a clear vision of your dream
evolving in front of you, you will be just
chasing with blurry vision.

Identifying all begins with this inner vision.
In order to get a clear vision you have to see it
from within. The third eye or inner mind has to
be awakened as most mystics would refer it to
as the mystical portal of your inner self.

Let's face it; the actual dream that you're
chasing is yourself. So to identify this dream of

yours it will take sometime. This is when the inner eye of your mind can see that dream. So every time you close your eyes, when your dream is no longer blurry and fully clear then you can see it even when your eyes are open. This is the process of evolving that vision into reality.

I once heard in a movie that I was watching called KICKBOXER 2 The Road Back. The character's name is David Sloan played by Sasha Mitchell he said in this movie

"Sometimes when you're blind and times seem darkest you could often see things more clearly."

David Sloan

TEST TIME:

Stop reading for just one moment, and close your eyes and envision who you want to become or how you want your life to be.

Write down on a separate sheet of paper what it is that you saw.

Now I could only imagine that it came to you fairly quickly. But at a cost, if you saw within your vision someone else such as a famous movie star, athlete, author, doctor, artists, musician, producer, lawyer, judge, business owner, ect....... Then that is okay.

Your vision will soon become clear at the end of this book that I can assure you. Once you can finally see you and only you in that dream of who you are about to become your

DON'T CHASE YOUR
DREAMS CATCH THEM

journey to catching it will be quicker than you think.

The only way to really capture that identity is to see it, feel it, believe in it, and then become it. Once this happens nothing will stop you from finding your identity. For really your dream is your identity. It is the perfect reflection of a life that awaits you and only you.

They are not two separate things they are one and the same thing. Throughout your life you will find that as young adolescents' that is what we try to find out these questions of who we are? What is our place in the world? What we are meant to do in our lives? The importance of what it is and what we could share, develop, learn, and become is the lingering questions that we have to answer by identifying with them.

There is actually one place that when you feel your dream there; it will be really easy for you to identify that dream. This place is in your gut; you see your gut will give you all the clues to finding that dream. I like to call this ___the knowing!___

This place is where all truth is held. The truth of the matter is your dream is your ultimate truth for you and only you. To know one's self is to know that dream. Through this process of identifying that dream of yours you have to locate the catapult. To launch it into new levels, new heights, new destinations, and new possibilities.

Once we have launched off the ground and into the stars we can begin to know our purpose, plus ourselves. Until then we stay on the ground looking and relating to our dream. In order to truly identify this dream we have to sort out the ones that hold us to the ground.

DON'T CHASE YOUR
DREAMS CATCH THEM

We all have a particular dream that were after. So you have to put a target on the one's you want the most in your life. But the target must have a bull's eye for you to make your mark on that dream. This is your way to identify with it. It is the only way to zero in on it and get a clear shot at it. To better understand what I'm trying to convey to you I'll put it to you this way.

Imagine that you are an arrow getting shot from a bow in order for that arrow (you); to hit the target the person (you); has to have a steady hand and clear vision of where the bull's eye is. If you have ever seen an archer you don't see them holding the bow with unsettling hands and they're surely not pointing the arrow in the opposite direction of the bulls' eye target.

To master this bull's eye target concept we have to hold onto our dreams with exact precision to nail the target in the center every time, when we let that arrow go.

This is called centering yourself. Everyone has heard about his or her center and if you haven't then let me introduce it to you. To centering ones self in life this is the concept for nailing the bull's eye head on every time. Without centering your vision you will go off the wrong path to identifying what it is that you want from your dream. You have to understand the center before you can proceed to identifying with this dream. Your center works like this every center has a straight line and a point at the end of that center. Like this:

DON'T CHASE YOUR
DREAMS CATCH THEM

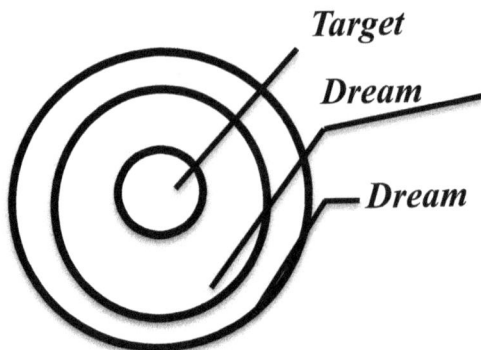

If you notice that the line is straight and pointing right at the center of the target, and with the lines are not, they both have made an angle within there lines and they where unable to hit the center. If you don't center yourself in your dream it will be hard for you to define it.

Being center means that your mind is clear of distractions and your focal point is straight on its target. That is when you know that you have defined what your dream is all about. I call these ***defining moments*** in your life. If you aren't centered then you will miss out on your chances to even notice when that moment comes.

This is what the adolescent years do for us. We go to school to become something are to try to define what it is; that we want to become. I know everyone remembers career day when all the children would bring someone to their school whether it was mom, dad, uncle, aunt, grandparents, brother, or sister; so they could talk about what career they had. That is where you would find out options to what you could become. I mean you could do anything and become anybody you wanted to become. It is always interesting to find a spark of interest when looking into who you want to become. Below I'll tell you what my beginning stages of sparks of interest were and where it all began.

DON'T CHASE YOUR
DREAMS CATCH THEM

THE BEGINNING OF

SPARKS OF INTEREST

Let me tell you that spark of interest could come from anywhere and from anyone all you have to do is to be centered in your life in order to define that spark within you and listen to it. I found my initial dream from one my best friends of mine that had realized my dream before I even saw it. Kenny Gehring had read a letter that I had wrote to a girl back in high school and he said to me "forget about being a model or an actor become an author." Shrugging it off and telling him that "I would never become an author" that is what I had said to him at that time.

For he saw the potential from me becoming an author initially knowing I had something to offer others. I didn't at the time because of other visions blocking my initial dream. This happened to me because not being centered in my life. But that spark of interest didn't come until years later. It actually happened when I was about to get out of the military and trying to find out what I was going to do and trying to identify my dream for myself. I found myself not realizing my dream for almost twelve years later after that conversion that my friend and me had on that day.

That is when I was still in search of identifying my dream for myself. I came to hear that spark of interest when I replayed that scenario in my head once more; and told myself that is what I wanted to do. My reason for telling you this story in the first place is for you to understand about listening intently, and how it helps you when finding out what dreams you are trying to identify with.

Remember I said your spark of interest can come from anywhere at anytime like mine

DON'T CHASE YOUR
DREAMS CATCH THEM

came 14 years before I knew it from my friend
Kenny. So if you are centered in your life you
will always be able to listen to your inner
dream intently no matter what.

Now coming from that spark of interest I
realized in order to identify that dream you
have to make a conscious thought about what
that dream is with inside you. You also have to
love everything about that dream in order not to
lose it in your subconscious.

This is what happened to me when I was
trying to search for my dream and identify it for
myself. I lost my dream back then because of
me not loving that dream and not being
centered. So that is why when doing your best
to identify your dream it is extremely important
to be centered and focus with it.

Now down below and on the next few
pages I have made a rating list of dreams and

you should rate them 0 thru 10 to help you with the identification process that you are on right now. Yes; I know what you are probably "thinking" why would I start off a rating list with zero?

Everything begins with zero; something always comes out of nothing. Nothingness is the void of something that is missing within your life; all you have to do is fill in the gap. So that is why I made the rating system for the identification process to start out with zero. This system is just a list of things I believe someone could possibly identify with.

To help them catch their own dream this is why I created it. So my apologies for it's lengthy introduction on the next 60 pages or so.

DON'T CHASE YOUR
DREAMS CATCH THEM

IDENTIFICATION RATING SYSTEM

PROCESS FOR YOUR DREAM

ACTRESS:

0 1 2 3 4 5 6 7 8 9 10

ACTOR:

0 1 2 3 4 5 6 7 8 9 10

AUTHOR:

0 1 2 3 4 5 6 7 8 9 10

ACUPUNTURIST:

0 1 2 3 4 5 6 7 8 9 10

AIR FLIGHT CONTROLLER:

0 1 2 3 4 5 6 7 8 9 10

ARMED FORCES MEMBER:

0 1 2 3 4 5 6 7 8 9 10

ACROBATIC:

0 1 2 3 4 5 6 7 8 9 10

ALCHEMIST:

0 1 2 3 4 5 6 7 8 9 10

AGRICULTURIST:

0 1 2 3 4 5 6 7 8 9 10

ANESTHESIOLOGIST:

0 1 2 3 4 5 6 7 8 9 10

ANNOUNCER:

0 1 2 3 4 5 6 7 8 9 10

ANTHROPOLOGIST:

0 1 2 3 4 5 6 7 8 9 10

ARCHAEOLOGIST:

0 1 2 3 4 5 6 7 8 9 10

ARACHNOLOGIST:

0 1 2 3 4 5 6 7 8 9 10

DON'T CHASE YOUR
DREAMS CATCH THEM

ARITHMETICIAN:

0 1 2 3 4 5 6 7 8 9 10

ARTIST:

0 1 2 3 4 5 6 7 8 9 10

ASTRONAUT:

0 1 2 3 4 5 6 7 8 9 10

ASTRONOMER:

0 1 2 3 4 5 6 7 8 9 10

ARCHITECT:

0 1 2 3 4 5 6 7 8 9 10

ARCHER:

0 1 2 3 4 5 6 7 8 9 10

ANTIQUE DEALER:

0 1 2 3 4 5 6 7 8 9 10

AUTO TRADER:

0 1 2 3 4 5 6 7 8 9 10

ANIMATOR:

0 1 2 3 4 5 6 7 8 9 10

AVIATOR:

0 1 2 3 4 5 6 7 8 9 10

AMBASSADOR:

0 1 2 3 4 5 6 7 8 9 10

ANCHOR MAN:

0 1 2 3 4 5 6 7 8 9 10

ANCHOR WOMAN:

0 1 2 3 4 5 6 7 8 9 10

AUDITOR:

0 1 2 3 4 5 6 7 8 9 10

AIKIDO MASTER:

0 1 2 3 4 5 6 7 8 9 10

BACTERIOLOGIST:

0 1 2 3 4 5 6 7 8 9 10

DON'T CHASE YOUR
DREAMS CATCH THEM

BOXER:

0 1 2 3 4 5 6 7 8 9 10

BANKER:

0 1 2 3 4 5 6 7 8 9 10

BARTENER:

0 1 2 3 4 5 6 7 8 9 10

BALLERINA:

0 1 2 3 4 5 6 7 8 9 10

BASEBALL PLAYER:

0 1 2 3 4 5 6 7 8 9 10

BASKETBALL PLAYER:

0 1 2 3 4 5 6 7 8 9 10

BEAUTICIAN:

0 1 2 3 4 5 6 7 8 9 10

BIOCHEMIST:

0 1 2 3 4 5 6 7 8 9 10

BIOENGINEER:

0 1 2 3 4 5 6 7 8 9 10

BIOLOGIST:

0 1 2 3 4 5 6 7 8 9 10

BODYGUARD:

0 1 2 3 4 5 6 7 8 9 10

BOOK KEEPER:

0 1 2 3 4 5 6 7 8 9 10

BOOK SELLER:

0 1 2 3 4 5 6 7 8 9 10

BOUNCER:

0 1 2 3 4 5 6 7 8 9 10

BOUNTY HUNTER:

0 1 2 3 4 5 6 7 8 9 10

BUSINESS OWNER:

0 1 2 3 4 5 6 7 8 9 10

*DON'T CHASE YOUR
DREAMS CATCH THEM*

BODYBUILDER:

0 1 2 3 4 5 6 7 8 9 10

BILLIONARE:

0 1 2 3 4 5 6 7 8 9 10

BUTLER:

0 1 2 3 4 5 6 7 8 9 10

BUTCHER:

0 1 2 3 4 5 6 7 8 9 10

BULL RIDER:

0 1 2 3 4 5 6 7 8 9 10

BIKER:

0 1 2 3 4 5 6 7 8 9 10

CAVE DIVER:

0 1 2 3 4 5 6 7 8 9 10

CAPTAIN:

0 1 2 3 4 5 6 7 8 9 10

CRAB CATCHER:

0 1 2 3 4 5 6 7 8 9 10

CHEMIST:

0 1 2 3 4 5 6 7 8 9 10

CHEERLEADER:

0 1 2 3 4 5 6 7 8 9 10

CHESS MASTER:

0 1 2 3 4 5 6 7 8 9 10

COOK:

0 1 2 3 4 5 6 7 8 9 10

CULINARY SPECIALIST:

0 1 2 3 4 5 6 7 8 9 10

CINEMATOGRAPHER:

0 1 2 3 4 5 6 7 8 9 10

CHIROPRACTOR:

0 1 2 3 4 5 6 7 8 9 10

*DON'T CHASE YOUR
DREAMS CATCH THEM*

CLAIRVOYANT:

0 1 2 3 4 5 6 7 8 9 10

COMEDIAN:

0 1 2 3 4 5 6 7 8 9 10

CONSTRUCTION WORKER:

0 1 2 3 4 5 6 7 8 9 10

CONDUCTOR:

0 1 2 3 4 5 6 7 8 9 10

COSMETOLOGIST:

0 1 2 3 4 5 6 7 8 9 10

COSMOLOGIST:

0 1 2 3 4 5 6 7 8 9 10

COUNSELOR:

0 1 2 3 4 5 6 7 8 9 10

COACH:

0 1 2 3 4 5 6 7 8 9 10

CRIMINOLOGIST:

0 1 2 3 4 5 6 7 8 9 10

CROCODILE HUNTER:

0 1 2 3 4 5 6 7 8 9 10

CLIMBER:

0 1 2 3 4 5 6 7 8 9 10

CLOWN:

0 1 2 3 4 5 6 7 8 9 10

CIRCUS PERFORMER:

0 1 2 3 4 5 6 7 8 9 10

COMMISSIONER:

0 1 2 3 4 5 6 7 8 9 10

COMPOSER:

0 1 2 3 4 5 6 7 8 9 10

CONGRESSMAN:

0 1 2 3 4 5 6 7 8 9 10

*DON'T CHASE YOUR
DREAMS CATCH THEM*

CONGRESSWOMEN:

0 1 2 3 4 5 6 7 8 9 10

COMIC WRITER:

0 1 2 3 4 5 6 7 8 9 10

CORONER:

0 1 2 3 4 5 6 7 8 9 10

CIA AGENT:

0 1 2 3 4 5 6 7 8 9 10

CHOREOGRAPHER:

0 1 2 3 4 5 6 7 8 9 10

CARPENTER:

0 1 2 3 4 5 6 7 8 9 10

CAKE DECORATOR:

0 1 2 3 4 5 6 7 8 9 10

COMPUTER TECHICIAN:

0 1 2 3 4 5 6 7 8 9 10

COMPUTER ENGINEER:

0 1 2 3 4 5 6 7 8 9 10

COMPUTER ANALYSIS:

0 1 2 3 4 5 6 7 8 9 10

DOCTOR:

0 1 2 3 4 5 6 7 8 9 10

DANCER:

0 1 2 3 4 5 6 7 8 9 10

DENTIST:

0 1 2 3 4 5 6 7 8 9 10

DELIVERY DRIVER:

0 1 2 3 4 5 6 7 8 9 10

DEEP SEA DIVER:

0 1 2 3 4 5 6 7 8 9 10

DERMATOLOGIST:

0 1 2 3 4 5 6 7 8 9 10

DON'T CHASE YOUR
DREAMS CATCH THEM

DIPLOMAT:

0 1 2 3 4 5 6 7 8 9 10

DISTRICT ATTORNEY:

0 1 2 3 4 5 6 7 8 9 10

DISTRIBUTOR:

0 1 2 3 4 5 6 7 8 9 10

DRAG RACER:

0 1 2 3 4 5 6 7 8 9 10

DEMONOLOGIST:

0 1 2 3 4 5 6 7 8 9 10

DEVELOPER:

0 1 2 3 4 5 6 7 8 9 10

DEPUTY:

0 1 2 3 4 5 6 7 8 9 10

DEPORTER:

0 1 2 3 4 5 6 7 8 9 10

DRAFTMAN:

0 1 2 3 4 5 6 7 8 9 10

DARE DEVIL:

0 1 2 3 4 5 6 7 8 9 10

DECIPHER:

0 1 2 3 4 5 6 7 8 9 10

DECORATOR:

0 1 2 3 4 5 6 7 8 9 10

DISPATCHER:

0 1 2 3 4 5 6 7 8 9 10

DIETICIAN:

0 1 2 3 4 5 6 7 8 9 10

DIRECTOR:

0 1 2 3 4 5 6 7 8 9 10

DOG TRAINER:

0 1 2 3 4 5 6 7 8 9 10

DON'T CHASE YOUR
DREAMS CATCH THEM

EDUCATOR:

0 1 2 3 4 5 6 7 8 9 10

EDITOR:

0 1 2 3 4 5 6 7 8 9 10

ENVIROMENTALIST:

0 1 2 3 4 5 6 7 8 9 10

ELECTRICIAN:

0 1 2 3 4 5 6 7 8 9 10

ENGINEER:

0 1 2 3 4 5 6 7 8 9 10

ENGRAVER:

0 1 2 3 4 5 6 7 8 9 10

ENTERTAINER:

0 1 2 3 4 5 6 7 8 9 10

ENTREPRENUER:

0 1 2 3 4 5 6 7 8 9 10

EQUESTRIAN:

0 1 2 3 4 5 6 7 8 9 10

EXHIBITOR:

0 1 2 3 4 5 6 7 8 9 10

EXHIBITIONIST:

0 1 2 3 4 5 6 7 8 9 10

EXECUTOR:

0 1 2 3 4 5 6 7 8 9 10

EXTREME JUMPER

0 1 2 3 4 5 6 7 8 9 10

EXPLORER:

0 1 2 3 4 5 6 7 8 9 10

EXTRACTOR:

0 1 2 3 4 5 6 7 8 9 10

FARMER:

0 1 2 3 4 5 6 7 8 9 10

*DON'T CHASE YOUR
DREAMS CATCH THEM*

FATHER:

0 1 2 3 4 5 6 7 8 9 10

FIREFIGHTER:

0 1 2 3 4 5 6 7 8 9 10

FISHERMEN:

0 1 2 3 4 5 6 7 8 9 10

FIGURE SKATER:

0 1 2 3 4 5 6 7 8 9 10

FLORIST:

0 1 2 3 4 5 6 7 8 9 10

FOOTBALL PLAYER:

0 1 2 3 4 5 6 7 8 9 10

FORECASTER:

0 1 2 3 4 5 6 7 8 9 10

FOREMAN:

0 1 2 3 4 5 6 7 8 9 10

FORENSIC SCIENTIST:

0 1 2 3 4 5 6 7 8 9 10

FORTUNE TELLER:

0 1 2 3 4 5 6 7 8 9 10

FRANCHISE OWNER:

0 1 2 3 4 5 6 7 8 9 10

FUMIGATOR:

0 1 2 3 4 5 6 7 8 9 10

FINANCIAL ADVISOR:

0 1 2 3 4 5 6 7 8 9 10

FREEMASON:

0 1 2 3 4 5 6 7 8 9 10

FASHION DESIGNER:

0 1 2 3 4 5 6 7 8 9 10

FRONTIER:

0 1 2 3 4 5 6 7 8 9 10

DON'T CHASE YOUR
DREAMS CATCH THEM

FUNDAMENTALIST:

0 1 2 3 4 5 6 7 8 9 10

FOOD CRITIC:

0 1 2 3 4 5 6 7 8 9 10

GEOGRAPHER:

0 1 2 3 4 5 6 7 8 9 10

GAMER:

0 1 2 3 4 5 6 7 8 9 10

GARDNER:

0 1 2 3 4 5 6 7 8 9 10

GEOCHEMIST:

0 1 2 3 4 5 6 7 8 9 10

GEMOLOGIST:

0 1 2 3 4 5 6 7 8 9 10

GENEOLOGIST:

0 1 2 3 4 5 6 7 8 9 10

GENEALOGIST:

0 1 2 3 4 5 6 7 8 9 10

GEOPHYSICIST:

0 1 2 3 4 5 6 7 8 9 10

GENIUS:

0 1 2 3 4 5 6 7 8 9 10

GERONTOLOGIST:

0 1 2 3 4 5 6 7 8 9 10

GHOST HUNTER:

0 1 2 3 4 5 6 7 8 9 10

GOVERNER:

0 1 2 3 4 5 6 7 8 9 10

GOSPEL SINGER:

0 1 2 3 4 5 6 7 8 9 10

GRAPHOLOGIST:

0 1 2 3 4 5 6 7 8 9 10

*DON'T CHASE YOUR
DREAMS CATCH THEM*

GRAPHIC DESIGNER:

0 1 2 3 4 5 6 7 8 9 10

GUARDIAN:

0 1 2 3 4 5 6 7 8 9 10

GYMNAST:

0 1 2 3 4 5 6 7 8 9 10

GYNECOLOGIST:

0 1 2 3 4 5 6 7 8 9 10

GYPSY:

0 1 2 3 4 5 6 7 8 9 10

GUITARIST:

0 1 2 3 4 5 6 7 8 9 10

GUARDSMAN:

0 1 2 3 4 5 6 7 8 9 10

GRADUTE:

0 1 2 3 4 5 6 7 8 9 10

GOLFER:

0 1 2 3 4 5 6 7 8 9 10

HEAD HUNTER:

0 1 2 3 4 5 6 7 8 9 10

HAIR DRESSER:

0 1 2 3 4 5 6 7 8 9 10

HORSE TRAINER:

0 1 2 3 4 5 6 7 8 9 10

HAIR STYLIST:

0 1 2 3 4 5 6 7 8 9 10

HANDY MAN:

0 1 2 3 4 5 6 7 8 9 10

HOME DECORATER:

0 1 2 3 4 5 6 7 8 9 10

HERBALIST:

0 1 2 3 4 5 6 7 8 9 10

DON'T CHASE YOUR
DREAMS CATCH THEM

HOUSE KEEPER:

0 1 2 3 4 5 6 7 8 9 10

HELMSMAN:

0 1 2 3 4 5 6 7 8 9 10

HERO:

0 1 2 3 4 5 6 7 8 9 10

HIKER:

0 1 2 3 4 5 6 7 8 9 10

HISTORIAN:

0 1 2 3 4 5 6 7 8 9 10

HUNTER:

0 1 2 3 4 5 6 7 8 9 10

HORSEMAN:

0 1 2 3 4 5 6 7 8 9 10

HOROLOGIST:

0 1 2 3 4 5 6 7 8 9 10

HYGIENIST:

0 1 2 3 4 5 6 7 8 9 10

HYDROTHERAPIST:

0 1 2 3 4 5 6 7 8 9 10

HYPNOTIST:

0 1 2 3 4 5 6 7 8 9 10

HYPNOTHERAPIST:

0 1 2 3 4 5 6 7 8 9 10

HOCKEY PLAYER:

0 1 2 3 4 5 6 7 8 9 10

ICE CREAM MAKER:

0 1 2 3 4 5 6 7 8 9 10

IDEOLOGIST:

0 1 2 3 4 5 6 7 8 9 10

ILLUSIONIST:

0 1 2 3 4 5 6 7 8 9 10

DON'T CHASE YOUR
DREAMS CATCH THEM

ILLUSTRATOR:

0 1 2 3 4 5 6 7 8 9 10

IMPERSONATOR:

0 1 2 3 4 5 6 7 8 9 10

IMPORTER:

0 1 2 3 4 5 6 7 8 9 10

INDEPENDENT:

0 1 2 3 4 5 6 7 8 9 10

INDUSTRIALIST:

0 1 2 3 4 5 6 7 8 9 10

INFORMER:

0 1 2 3 4 5 6 7 8 9 10

INFORMANT:

0 1 2 3 4 5 6 7 8 9 10

INN KEEPER:

0 1 2 3 4 5 6 7 8 9 10

INNOVATOR:

0 1 2 3 4 5 6 7 8 9 10

INSPECTOR:

0 1 2 3 4 5 6 7 8 9 10

INTERPRETER:

0 1 2 3 4 5 6 7 8 9 10

INVENTOR:

0 1 2 3 4 5 6 7 8 9 10

JANITOR:

0 1 2 3 4 5 6 7 8 9 10

JOCKEY:

0 1 2 3 4 5 6 7 8 9 10

JEWELER:

0 1 2 3 4 5 6 7 8 9 10

JUDGE:

0 1 2 3 4 5 6 7 8 9 10

DON'T CHASE YOUR
DREAMS CATCH THEM

JUGGLER:

0 1 2 3 4 5 6 7 8 9 10

JOURNALIST:

0 1 2 3 4 5 6 7 8 9 10

JUDO MASTER:

0 1 2 3 4 5 6 7 8 9 10

JUJITSU MASTER:

0 1 2 3 4 5 6 7 8 9 10

KEYBOARD PLAYER:

0 1 2 3 4 5 6 7 8 9 10

KUNG FU MASTER:

0 1 2 3 4 5 6 7 8 9 10

KARATE MASTER:

0 1 2 3 4 5 6 7 8 9 10

KNIGHT:

0 1 2 3 4 5 6 7 8 9 10

LACROSSE PLAYER:

0 1 2 3 4 5 6 7 8 9 10

LANDSCAPER:

0 1 2 3 4 5 6 7 8 9 10

LAW MAKER:

0 1 2 3 4 5 6 7 8 9 10

LAWYER:

0 1 2 3 4 5 6 7 8 9 10

LEGIONNAIRE:

0 1 2 3 4 5 6 7 8 9 10

LEGISLATOR:

0 1 2 3 4 5 6 7 8 9 10

LEGEND:

0 1 2 3 4 5 6 7 8 9 10

LINGERIE MODEL:

0 1 2 3 4 5 6 7 8 9 10

*DON'T CHASE YOUR
DREAMS CATCH THEM*

LINGUIST:

0 1 2 3 4 5 6 7 8 9 10

LIFE GUARD:

0 1 2 3 4 5 6 7 8 9 10

LIBRARIAN:

0 1 2 3 4 5 6 7 8 9 10

LIAISION:

0 1 2 3 4 5 6 7 8 9 10

LUMBER JACKER:

0 1 2 3 4 5 6 7 8 9 10

LIEUTENANT:

0 1 2 3 4 5 6 7 8 9 10

LEGACY:

0 1 2 3 4 5 6 7 8 9 10

LOTTERY WINNER:

0 1 2 3 4 5 6 7 8 9 10

LOBSTER CATCHER:

0 1 2 3 4 5 6 7 8 9 10

LYRICIST:

0 1 2 3 4 5 6 7 8 9 10

LOAN OFFICER:

0 1 2 3 4 5 6 7 8 9 10

MACHINIST:

0 1 2 3 4 5 6 7 8 9 10

MAGICIAN:

0 1 2 3 4 5 6 7 8 9 10

MAILMAN:

0 1 2 3 4 5 6 7 8 9 10

MAID:

0 1 2 3 4 5 6 7 8 9 10

MAKE UP ARTIST:

0 1 2 3 4 5 6 7 8 9 10

*DON'T CHASE YOUR
DREAMS CATCH THEM*

MANAGER:

0 1 2 3 4 5 6 7 8 9 10

MARKSMAN:

0 1 2 3 4 5 6 7 8 9 10

MARRIED:

0 1 2 3 4 5 6 7 8 9 10

MASSAGE THERAPIST:

0 1 2 3 4 5 6 7 8 9 10

MAYOR:

0 1 2 3 4 5 6 7 8 9 10

MARTIAL ARTIST:

0 1 2 3 4 5 6 7 8 9 10

MENTALIST:

0 1 2 3 4 5 6 7 8 9 10

MATHEMATICIAN:

0 1 2 3 4 5 6 7 8 9 10

MINER:

0 1 2 3 4 5 6 7 8 9 10

MECHANIC:

0 1 2 3 4 5 6 7 8 9 10

MEDALIST:

0 1 2 3 4 5 6 7 8 9 10

MEDITATOR:

0 1 2 3 4 5 6 7 8 9 10

MEDIUM:

0 1 2 3 4 5 6 7 8 9 10

MEDICINE MAN:

0 1 2 3 4 5 6 7 8 9 10

MENTOR:

0 1 2 3 4 5 6 7 8 9 10

MERCENARY:

0 1 2 3 4 5 6 7 8 9 10

DON'T CHASE YOUR
DREAMS CATCH THEM

MERCHANDISER:

0 1 2 3 4 5 6 7 8 9 10

METEOROLOGIST:

0 1 2 3 4 5 6 7 8 9 10

METHODOLOGIST:

0 1 2 3 4 5 6 7 8 9 10

MICROBIOLOGIST:

0 1 2 3 4 5 6 7 8 9 10

MILLIONAIRE:

0 1 2 3 4 5 6 7 8 9 10

METAPHYSICIAN:

0 1 2 3 4 5 6 7 8 9 10

MINISTER:

0 1 2 3 4 5 6 7 8 9 10

MINERALOGIST:

0 1 2 3 4 5 6 7 8 9 10

MODEL:

0 1 2 3 4 5 6 7 8 9 10

MONK:

0 1 2 3 4 5 6 7 8 9 10

MORTICIAN:

0 1 2 3 4 5 6 7 8 9 10

MOTHER:

0 1 2 3 4 5 6 7 8 9 10

MOTIVATIONAL SPEAKER:

0 1 2 3 4 5 6 7 8 9 10

MOTORCYCLIST:

0 1 2 3 4 5 6 7 8 9 10

MOUNTAINEER:

0 1 2 3 4 5 6 7 8 9 10

MOUNTAIN CLIMBER:

0 1 2 3 4 5 6 7 8 9 10

DON'T CHASE YOUR
DREAMS CATCH THEM

MYCOLOGIST:

0 1 2 3 4 5 6 7 8 9 10

MYTHOLOGIST:

0 1 2 3 4 5 6 7 8 9 10

MULTIMILLIONARE:

0 1 2 3 4 5 6 7 8 9 10

MMA FIGHTER:

0 1 2 3 4 5 6 7 8 9 10

NANNY:

0 1 2 3 4 5 6 7 8 9 10

NARRATOR:

0 1 2 3 4 5 6 7 8 9 10

NATIONALIST:

0 1 2 3 4 5 6 7 8 9 10

NAVIGATOR:

0 1 2 3 4 5 6 7 8 9 10

NINJA:

0 1 2 3 4 5 6 7 8 9 10

NEGOTIATOR:

0 1 2 3 4 5 6 7 8 9 10

NEUROLOGIST:

0 1 2 3 4 5 6 7 8 9 10

NEWSCASTER:

0 1 2 3 4 5 6 7 8 9 10

NOVELIST:

0 1 2 3 4 5 6 7 8 9 10

NURSE:

0 1 2 3 4 5 6 7 8 9 10

NUTRITIONIST:

0 1 2 3 4 5 6 7 8 9 10

OBSTRETRICIAN:

0 1 2 3 4 5 6 7 8 9 10

*DON'T CHASE YOUR
DREAMS CATCH THEM*

OCEANOGRAPHER:

0 1 2 3 4 5 6 7 8 9 10

OLYMPIAN:

0 1 2 3 4 5 6 7 8 9 10

OPERA SINGER:

0 1 2 3 4 5 6 7 8 9 10

OPERATOR:

0 1 2 3 4 5 6 7 8 9 10

OPHTHALMOLOGIST:

0 1 2 3 4 5 6 7 8 9 10

OPPORTUNIST:

0 1 2 3 4 5 6 7 8 9 10

ORGANIZER:

0 1 2 3 4 5 6 7 8 9 10

ORDAINER:

0 1 2 3 4 5 6 7 8 9 10

ORIGINATOR:

0 1 2 3 4 5 6 7 8 9 10

ORNITHOLOGIST:

0 1 2 3 4 5 6 7 8 9 10

ORTHODONIST:

0 1 2 3 4 5 6 7 8 9 10

ORTHOPEDIST:

0 1 2 3 4 5 6 7 8 9 10

OWNER:

0 1 2 3 4 5 6 7 8 9 10

PAGENT WINNER:

0 1 2 3 4 5 6 7 8 9 10

PAINTER:

0 1 2 3 4 5 6 7 8 9 10

PALEONTOLOGIST:

0 1 2 3 4 5 6 7 8 9 10

DON'T CHASE YOUR
DREAMS CATCH THEM

PALMIST:

0 1 2 3 4 5 6 7 8 9 10

PANELIST:

0 1 2 3 4 5 6 7 8 9 10

PARACHUTIST:

0 1 2 3 4 5 6 7 8 9 10

PARAMEDIC:

0 1 2 3 4 5 6 7 8 9 10

PASTOR:

0 1 2 3 4 5 6 7 8 9 10

PATHOLOGIST:

0 1 2 3 4 5 6 7 8 9 10

PARANORMAL INVESTIGATER:

0 1 2 3 4 5 6 7 8 9 10

PEDIATRICIAN:

0 1 2 3 4 5 6 7 8 9 10

PEDICURIST:

0 1 2 3 4 5 6 7 8 9 10

PERFORMER:

0 1 2 3 4 5 6 7 8 9 10

PHARMACIST:

0 1 2 3 4 5 6 7 8 9 10

PHARMACOLOGIST:

0 1 2 3 4 5 6 7 8 9 10

PHILANTHROPIST:

0 1 2 3 4 5 6 7 8 9 10

PHILOLOGIST:

0 1 2 3 4 5 6 7 8 9 10

PHILOSOPHER:

0 1 2 3 4 5 6 7 8 9 10

PHOTOGRAPHER:

0 1 2 3 4 5 6 7 8 9 10

DON'T CHASE YOUR
DREAMS CATCH THEM

PHYSICIST:

0 1 2 3 4 5 6 7 8 9 10

PHYSIOLOGIST:

0 1 2 3 4 5 6 7 8 9 10

PIANOIST:

0 1 2 3 4 5 6 7 8 9 10

PILOT:

0 1 2 3 4 5 6 7 8 9 10

PIRATE:

0 1 2 3 4 5 6 7 8 9 10

POKER PLAYER:

0 1 2 3 4 5 6 7 8 9 10

POLICE MAN/WOMEN:

0 1 2 3 4 5 6 7 8 9 10

POLITICIAN:

0 1 2 3 4 5 6 7 8 9 10

PAWN BROKER:

0 1 2 3 4 5 6 7 8 9 10

PRINCIPAL:

0 1 2 3 4 5 6 7 8 9 10

PRESIDENT:

0 1 2 3 4 5 6 7 8 9 10

PROFESSOR:

0 1 2 3 4 5 6 7 8 9 10

PROGRAMMER:

0 1 2 3 4 5 6 7 8 9 10

PRODUCER:

0 1 2 3 4 5 6 7 8 9 10

PROPHET:

0 1 2 3 4 5 6 7 8 9 10

PROOF READER:

0 1 2 3 4 5 6 7 8 9 10

DON'T CHASE YOUR
DREAMS CATCH THEM

PROPERTY OWNER:

0 1 2 3 4 5 6 7 8 9 10

PROSECUTER:

0 1 2 3 4 5 6 7 8 9 10

PROTECTOR:

0 1 2 3 4 5 6 7 8 9 10

PROVIDER:

0 1 2 3 4 5 6 7 8 9 10

PSYCHIC:

0 1 2 3 4 5 6 7 8 9 10

PSYCHOANALYST:

0 1 2 3 4 5 6 7 8 9 10

PSYCHOLOGIST:

0 1 2 3 4 5 6 7 8 9 10

PSYCHOPATHOLOGIST:

0 1 2 3 4 5 6 7 8 9 10

PSYCHOTHERAPIST:

0 1 2 3 4 5 6 7 8 9 10

PUBLICIST:

0 1 2 3 4 5 6 7 8 9 10

PUBLISHER:

0 1 2 3 4 5 6 7 8 9 10

PYROTECHNICIAN:

0 1 2 3 4 5 6 7 8 9 10

QUANTUM PHYSICIAN:

0 1 2 3 4 5 6 7 8 9 10

RACER:

0 1 2 3 4 5 6 7 8 9 10

RADIO HOST:

0 1 2 3 4 5 6 7 8 9 10

RADIOLOGIST:

0 1 2 3 4 5 6 7 8 9 10

DON'T CHASE YOUR
DREAMS CATCH THEM

RAPPER:

0 1 2 3 4 5 6 7 8 9 10

REMOTE VIEWER:

0 1 2 3 4 5 6 7 8 9 10

REALTOR:

0 1 2 3 4 5 6 7 8 9 10

RECRUITER:

0 1 2 3 4 5 6 7 8 9 10

REFEREE:

0 1 2 3 4 5 6 7 8 9 10

REPORTER:

0 1 2 3 4 5 6 7 8 9 10

SAGE:

0 1 2 3 4 5 6 7 8 9 10

SAILOR:

0 1 2 3 4 5 6 7 8 9 10

SALES PERSON:

0 1 2 3 4 5 6 7 8 9 10

SNAKE HUNTER:

0 1 2 3 4 5 6 7 8 9 10

SCHOLAR:

0 1 2 3 4 5 6 7 8 9 10

SCHOOL TEACHER:

0 1 2 3 4 5 6 7 8 9 10

SCIENTIST:

0 1 2 3 4 5 6 7 8 9 10

SCIENTOLOGIST:

0 1 2 3 4 5 6 7 8 9 10

SCOUT MASTER:

0 1 2 3 4 5 6 7 8 9 10

SCRIPT WRITER:

0 1 2 3 4 5 6 7 8 9 10

*DON'T CHASE YOUR
DREAMS CATCH THEM*

SCUBA DIVER:

0 1 2 3 4 5 6 7 8 9 10

SURFER:

0 1 2 3 4 5 6 7 8 9 10

SCULPTOR:

0 1 2 3 4 5 6 7 8 9 10

SECRETARY:

0 1 2 3 4 5 6 7 8 9 10

SECURITY GUARD:

0 1 2 3 4 5 6 7 8 9 10

SEISMOLOGIST:

0 1 2 3 4 5 6 7 8 9 10

SELF CONFIDENT:

0 1 2 3 4 5 6 7 8 9 10

SENATOR:

0 1 2 3 4 5 6 7 8 9 10

SERGEANT:

0 1 2 3 4 5 6 7 8 9 10

SHAMANIST:

0 1 2 3 4 5 6 7 8 9 10

SHERIFF:

0 1 2 3 4 5 6 7 8 9 10

SHOE MAKER:

0 1 2 3 4 5 6 7 8 9 10

SHOPPER:

0 1 2 3 4 5 6 7 8 9 10

SINGER:

0 1 2 3 4 5 6 7 8 9 10

SKIER:

0 1 2 3 4 5 6 7 8 9 10

SKY DIVER:

0 1 2 3 4 5 6 7 8 9 10

DON'T CHASE YOUR
DREAMS CATCH THEM

SKATER:

0 1 2 3 4 5 6 7 8 9 10

SLENDER:

0 1 2 3 4 5 6 7 8 9 10

SOCCER:

0 1 2 3 4 5 6 7 8 9 10

SOCIALIST:

0 1 2 3 4 5 6 7 8 9 10

SOCIOLOGIST:

0 1 2 3 4 5 6 7 8 9 10

SNIPER:

0 1 2 3 4 5 6 7 8 9 10

SORCERER:

0 1 2 3 4 5 6 7 8 9 10

SPECIALIST:

0 1 2 3 4 5 6 7 8 9 10

SPORTS CASTER:

0 1 2 3 4 5 6 7 8 9 10

SPOKENSMAN:

0 1 2 3 4 5 6 7 8 9 10

SPOKENSWOMEN:

0 1 2 3 4 5 6 7 8 9 10

SPIRITUALIST:

0 1 2 3 4 5 6 7 8 9 10

STATESMAN:

0 1 2 3 4 5 6 7 8 9 10

STOCK BROKER:

0 1 2 3 4 5 6 7 8 9 10

STORY TELLER:

0 1 2 3 4 5 6 7 8 9 10

STEWARDEST:

0 1 2 3 4 5 6 7 8 9 10

*DON'T CHASE YOUR
DREAMS CATCH THEM*

STRATEGIST:

0 1 2 3 4 5 6 7 8 9 10

STUNT PERSON:

0 1 2 3 4 5 6 7 8 9 10

SUPERHUMAN:

0 1 2 3 4 5 6 7 8 9 10

SUPERINTENDENT:

0 1 2 3 4 5 6 7 8 9 10

SUPERVISOR:

0 1 2 3 4 5 6 7 8 9 10

SUPPLIER:

0 1 2 3 4 5 6 7 8 9 10

SUPPORTER:

0 1 2 3 4 5 6 7 8 9 10

SNOW BOARDER

0 1 2 3 4 5 6 7 8 9 10

SWIMMER:

0 1 2 3 4 5 6 7 8 9 10

SWORDSMAN:

0 1 2 3 4 5 6 7 8 9 10

TATTO ARTIST:

0 1 2 3 4 5 6 7 8 9 10

TANTRIC MASTER:

0 1 2 3 4 5 6 7 8 9 10

TECHNICIAN:

0 1 2 3 4 5 6 7 8 9 10

TEACHER:

0 1 2 3 4 5 6 7 8 9 10

TENNIS PLAYER

0 1 2 3 4 5 6 7 8 9 10

*DON'T CHASE YOUR
DREAMS CATCH THEM*

TECHNOLOGIST:

0 1 2 3 4 5 6 7 8 9 10

TELECASTER:

0 1 2 3 4 5 6 7 8 9 10

TELLEPATHIST:

0 1 2 3 4 5 6 7 8 9 10

TELEPROMPTER:

0 1 2 3 4 5 6 7 8 9 10

TELEVISION HOST:

0 1 2 3 4 5 6 7 8 9 10

TELEVISION PRODUCER:

0 1 2 3 4 5 6 7 8 9 10

THEORIST:

0 1 2 3 4 5 6 7 8 9 10

THERAPIST:

0 1 2 3 4 5 6 7 8 9 10

TOOL MAKER:

0 1 2 3 4 5 6 7 8 9 10

TOUR GUIDE:

0 1 2 3 4 5 6 7 8 9 10

TOXICOLOGIST:

0 1 2 3 4 5 6 7 8 9 10

TRADESMAN:

0 1 2 3 4 5 6 7 8 9 10

TRANSCRIBER:

0 1 2 3 4 5 6 7 8 9 10

TRANSPORTER:

0 1 2 3 4 5 6 7 8 9 10

TREASURE HUNTER:

0 1 2 3 4 5 6 7 8 9 10

TREASURER:

0 1 2 3 4 5 6 7 8 9 10

*DON'T CHASE YOUR
DREAMS CATCH THEM*

THERORIZER:

0 1 2 3 4 5 6 7 8 9 10

TOPOGRAPHER:

0 1 2 3 4 5 6 7 8 9 10

TOURIST:

0 1 2 3 4 5 6 7 8 9 10

TOXICOLOGIST:

0 1 2 3 4 5 6 7 8 9 10

TRADITIONALIST:

0 1 2 3 4 5 6 7 8 9 10

TRAMPOLINIST:

0 1 2 3 4 5 6 7 8 9 10

TRANSCRIBER:

0 1 2 3 4 5 6 7 8 9 10

TRANSLATOR:

0 1 2 3 4 5 6 7 8 9 10

TRIBESMEN:

0 1 2 3 4 5 6 7 8 9 10

TROUBLE SHOOTER:

0 1 2 3 4 5 6 7 8 9 10

TYPOGRAPHER:

0 1 2 3 4 5 6 7 8 9 10

UMPIRE:

0 1 2 3 4 5 6 7 8 9 10

US CITIZEN:

0 1 2 3 4 5 6 7 8 9 10

UNDERWRITER:

0 1 2 3 4 5 6 7 8 9 10

UNIONIST:

0 1 2 3 4 5 6 7 8 9 10

UNIQUE:

0 1 2 3 4 5 6 7 8 9 10

DON'T CHASE YOUR
DREAMS CATCH THEM

VACILLATOR:

0 1 2 3 4 5 6 7 8 9 10

VAULTER:

0 1 2 3 4 5 6 7 8 9 10

VEGETARIAN:

0 1 2 3 4 5 6 7 8 9 10

VENDOR:

0 1 2 3 4 5 6 7 8 9 10

VENTRILOQUIST:

0 1 2 3 4 5 6 7 8 9 10

VETERINARIAN:

0 1 2 3 4 5 6 7 8 9 10

VICE ADMIRAL:

0 1 2 3 4 5 6 7 8 9 10

VICE CHANCELLOR:

0 1 2 3 4 5 6 7 8 9 10

VICE PRESIDENT:

0 1 2 3 4 5 6 7 8 9 10

VICTOR:

0 1 2 3 4 5 6 7 8 9 10

VIGILANTE:

0 1 2 3 4 5 6 7 8 9 10

VINDICATOR:

0 1 2 3 4 5 6 7 8 9 10

VIOLINIST:

0 1 2 3 4 5 6 7 8 9 10

VIROLOGIST:

0 1 2 3 4 5 6 7 8 9 10

VOCALIST:

0 1 2 3 4 5 6 7 8 9 10

VOLLEY BALL PLAYER:

0 1 2 3 4 5 6 7 8 9 10

*DON'T CHASE YOUR
DREAMS CATCH THEM*

VOODOOIST:

0 1 2 3 4 5 6 7 8 9 10

VOYAGER:

0 1 2 3 4 5 6 7 8 9 10

WAITER:

0 1 2 3 4 5 6 7 8 9 10

WAITRESS:

0 1 2 3 4 5 6 7 8 9 10

WARDEN:

0 1 2 3 4 5 6 7 8 9 10

WARRIOR:

0 1 2 3 4 5 6 7 8 9 10

WEATHERFORECASTER:

0 1 2 3 4 5 6 7 8 9 10

WEB DESIGNER:

0 1 2 3 4 5 6 7 8 9 10

WEIGHT LIFTER:

0 1 2 3 4 5 6 7 8 9 10

WIELDER:

0 1 2 3 4 5 6 7 8 9 10

WITCH:

0 1 2 3 4 5 6 7 8 9 10

WIZARD:

0 1 2 3 4 5 6 7 8 9 10

WINE MAKER:

0 1 2 3 4 5 6 7 8 9 10

WRESTLER:

0 1 2 3 4 5 6 7 8 9 10

WRITER:

0 1 2 3 4 5 6 7 8 9 10

X-RAY TECHINCIAN:

0 1 2 3 4 5 6 7 8 9 10

DON'T CHASE YOUR
DREAMS CATCH THEM

XYLOPHONIST:

0 1 2 3 4 5 6 7 8 9 10

YACHTSMAN:

0 1 2 3 4 5 6 7 8 9 10

YOGA MASTER:

0 1 2 3 4 5 6 7 8 9 10

ZODIAC READER:

0 1 2 3 4 5 6 7 8 9 10

ZOO KEEPER:

0 1 2 3 4 5 6 7 8 9 10

ZOOLOGIST:

0 1 2 3 4 5 6 7 8 9 10

Now it is my hope that with this list it will help you in the identification process, and give you a spark of interest. Think of it has your personal career day from your school but in this book.

Remember if you listen intently and you become centered in your life, you will be able to identify your dream that much more easier. Now it is okay to change your dream. If you can go to the place where you are centered, your vision won't be blurry and it should be clear. That is when you know you're on your way to the big catch.

DON'T CHASE YOUR
DREAMS CATCH THEM

CHAPTER TWO

RUNAWAY THOUGHTS

Now once you have identified what your dream is; you have to be aware of runaway thoughts. These runaway thoughts can be dangerous to your developing dream. Once these runaway thoughts begin it is hard to catch up to them once you have begun the chase.

Catching up to your runaway thoughts or collective thoughts can be difficult. You see when your thoughts are on the run, your mind stores them in your subconscious. Within the hassle & bustle of the traffic jams within your mind, you will go to places that take you to unusual turns and shifts in your life. Once this happens to you; those thoughts, which have might of been so clear to you at that time; will

DON'T CHASE YOUR
DREAMS CATCH THEM

go on the runaway train within your mind, which you have to get caught up too.

That is when the race is on within your mind. When a thought has runaway from its place of origin it might take sometime to catch up to it. That thought will make you go on a wild goose chase for it.

A simple explanation of a runaway thought is this. You see we have runaway thoughts every day. They work like this; a *"surge of brilliance"* will take place in your mind. This surge of brilliance is most likely to be your dream of dreams attempting to get your attention. Once this surge of brilliance reaches and calls out to you we have to take note of it. If we don't take note of it, it could be lost in the fragment battlefield of our mind.

All these other thoughts will rush in and make that one pointed thought or surge of

brilliance runaway from that moment. It is
when that light bulb goes off in your head and
everything is as clear as day. But it happens so
fast that this light bulb moment could go off as
quickly as it turned on. So once it's on is when
you can feel your surge of brilliance happening.
Once that light bulb starts to go dim is when
you know that initial light bulb thought is on
the run.

That one pointed thought will runaway into
your subconscious and will be suppressed into
your mind. It will affect the process of catching
your dream. All of these other thoughts will
block the surge of brilliance to where it will lay
dormant within your subconscious.

In order to prevent this dormant feeling that
you will get from this loss of action from other
thoughts entering your mind. You will have to
notice that your runaway thought will also slow
down your progress to catching this surge of

DON'T CHASE YOUR
DREAMS CATCH THEM

brilliance that lies within you. So I have put on the next few pages a counter action to this loss of your own, surge of brilliance.

I call it the ***stroke of genius list****; this list will allow you to keep your **surge of brilliance** close by. It will enable you to keep that runaway thought out of your subconscious in order to access it when it is needed.* This technique will allow you to make everything easier when you're in the planning stages of the big catch.

STROKE OF GENIUS LIST!!!!!

_____

_____

_____

_____

_____

_____

_____

_____

_____

_____

DON'T CHASE YOUR
DREAMS CATCH THEM

DON'T CHASE YOUR
DREAMS CATCH THEM

_____

_____

_____

_____

_____

_____

_____

_____

_____

_____

_____

_____

_____

_____

_____

*DON'T CHASE YOUR
DREAMS CATCH THEM*

_____

_____

_____

_____

_____

_____

_____

_____

_____

_____

_____

_____

_____

_____

_____

_____

_____

_____

_____

_____

_____

_____

_____

_____

_____

_____

_____

_____

DON'T CHASE YOUR
DREAMS CATCH THEM

The stroke of genius list will help you with the catch. This stroke of genius list is equivalent to the light bulb that goes off in your head when having an inspiring thought. So when the light bulb goes off, write it down in order to make it part of your stroke of genius list.

Don't wait to write it down, write it down right away as soon as it strikes your mind. For your surge of brilliance will strike your mind like a bolt of lighting coming down from the heavens. It will go along way, in combating with your run away thought, and because once it has run away from your mind into your subconscious mind, it will take some time to retrieve it.

It helps you not to forget what your inspired thought was. Remember when in the middle of the chase for your dream you have to do what ever you can to protect it. That is the only way you will be able to catch that dream of yours. Along the way of your chase it is imperative that you keep your *stroke of genius list* with you at all times. Whether you use the list in the book or you make your own list or have a personal journal.

With this technique those thoughts will no longer be *run away thoughts* they will be *captured thoughts* and that is the idea to capture your *surge of brilliance* with a simple *stroke of genius!!!*

DON'T CHASE YOUR
DREAMS CATCH THEM

CHAPTER THREE

HIDE AND SEEK

"It's not about how many attempts it takes, it's about never giving up until it happens."

Sean Alexander Hamilton

Now at this stage in the chase it is exactly what the title entails the hide and seek method. I want you; for one moment, to imagine and take yourself back to the game of *hide and seek* that you once used to play as a child. I'll have to tell you this is what is going

*DON'T CHASE YOUR
DREAMS CATCH THEM*

on with your dream. But unknown to you and your conscious mind isn't latching on because the sub conscious steps in.

THE SEEKER

You're the seeker, but your dream is hiding from you. Now if you go back to when you were a kid that was the counters job, who after finished counting became the seeker in the game of *hide and seek.* When the game was played in your neighborhood, the seeker knew from the start of the game, it wasn't over until the last kid was found. Well that is the same concept here that you have to take with your *DREAM.* The hunt for your dream isn't over until it is found and caught.

When your dream is in hiding you have to become the seeker for that dream. Now when you are seeking that dream of yours you have to do three things:

1. *Look: looking for that dream through the mind's portal and seeing it come into realization through visualization!*

2. *Listen: hearing with your inner spirit and understanding where this voice in your mind is coming from?*

3. *Learn: learning how to get there through the D methods, which I will explain these methods, in the next few pages.*

But before that I will go over a few more concepts. Now these questions you will not answer in that order and not all at the same time.

When you are looking for that dream you are looking for clues to your dream. Just has you will in the game of *hide and seek.* You start to track down these clues that are left behind from your attempts into finding the dream within your mind's portal.

Without the clues your job as a tracker can become hopeless, your tracking capabilities are useless at this point in the game and your dream could be jeopardized. In life we will all have clues that lead us into our dreams. It is as if you are finding clues to find someone in the game of *hide and seek.* Remember when you where looking for some one, you would try to look for clues such as a broken branch in the woods are a footprint that was left in the sand to find that person.

Once you find your way through the portal of your mind through the looking glass of your visual cortex theses moments of blurred vision will come into view. You will be able to see the realization of your dream come out of hiding. Then you'll know what path to take to get there faster than you could ever imaged.

The next step to being a good tracker of your dream in this game of *hide and seek* is to listen closely and very intently to the inner voice of your mind. The inner voice of yours will speak to you about your dream very often throughout your life. It doesn't matter what stage or where you are in your life if you listen to that inner voice that screams out to you.

Then you will hear everything clearly about that dream of yours. At this moment in the stage of the *hide and seek* game it is simply called the *CALLING*. You have to listen for your inner calling for it will call out to you when you listen intently and closely for it.

THE CALLING

The inner small voice within you is called the calling. It's equivalent to a dog whistle that only dogs can hear. That's what it is to every individual out there. The calling can only be heard by your inner voice. I can't tell you when that moment of the calling will happen for you. But I can tell you it will happen. It just might happen when you're completely lost and unsure about your life. But you will know when it's your calling moment.

The final step is learning about this dream through the D methods. Which I call the eight ultimate **(D's)** they entail.

DON'T CHASE YOUR
DREAMS CATCH THEM

1. D number one is **Decision**: To come up with a decisive plan and make action steps towards that deciding factor that will lead you into catching that dream.

2. D number two is **Determination**: To never stop seeking your dream and to find the right resources to keep you going to get what you want in your dream. Also to not let anything get in your way. The process of establishing something exactly by calculation or research.

3. D number three is **Drive:** To keep you going to get what you want in your dream. Using this concept of failure is the process by accepting it and driving through the obstacles

that stand in your way. To propel or carry along by force in a specified direction.

4. D number four is **Dedication:** Staying on course even after the feeling of enthusiasm as left your heart, body, and mind. Committed to a task or purpose.

5. D number five is **Developing:** Is the process of expanding your knowledge, wisdom, and expertise, in the subject field. It's on the form of growing through expansion in all fields of the process to becoming more mature, advanced, or elaborate in your selective vision of your dream.

6. D number six is **Discipline:** Is the act of controlling ones behavior to achieving a specific outcome or end result, or a habitual way of lifestyle changes to meeting your dreams in your daily activities in reality base foundations of action movements.

7. D number seven is **Doing:** Is the act of taking calculated steps and movements in activities to get to your dream destination. Keeping engagement with your evolving vision on a conscious level to being able to gage end result performances.

8. D number eight is **Due Date:** This gives us a targeted goal and holds us accountable to the actions we're taking to reach that goal.

This is the game of *hide and seek* you are the seeker and your dream is the one doing the hiding. So this is what you need to do to become a successful seeker in your journey or quest for the dream that lives within you. Remember I want you to become the ultimate seeker. A seeker that finds the one thing that is hiding.

You can be the ultimate seeker by following the D methods. Remember it is all about making the **decision**, finding the **determination**, staying **driven**, by being

dedicated, seeking to **develop** your strengths along with your weaknesses, by **disciplining** yourself through the process of tracking results, through action steps in **doing** and making a **due date** to reach your final destination. *Your ULTIMATE DREAM whatever it might be.*

If you noticed that if your reading this book right now you're already an ultimate seeker. Something that was within you made you look for a book just like this. You where already seeking something to take you to where you need to be. So I sure hope this will be your last stop.

*DON'T CHASE YOUR
DREAMS CATCH THEM*

CHAPTER FOUR

TREADMILL EFFECT

Now the majority of you have seen and been on a treadmill before. What you are probably not aware of is that you're still on that treadmill. Now when you are on a treadmill you don't see what you're missing in your life. Most treadmills are inside of gyms or in homes and we lose the beauty of what could be seen from outside of this element.

We get stuck in this element and that is why I call it the ***treadmill effect***. The treadmill effect works as such; it loses all of its advantages as well as your glory to the ultimate goal. Throughout your life and in your quest for your dream the only way to catch it is to get off of the treadmill and go make it happen. You need to step outside of your self and your natural comfort zone to escape the treadmill effect.

Now the treadmill effect is easy to get stuck on due to some out of your comfort zone phobias. Some of you might say "well I like getting on the treadmill every morning." If you get off the treadmill, who knows what lies ahead of you?

The treadmill holds you back from your full potential. We don't escape from it because of phobias such as the fear of being seen when walking or running outside. People that have phobias such as wondering how other people are going to judge them are what keep them on the treadmill. They have questions such as;

DON'T CHASE YOUR
DREAMS CATCH THEM

WHAT IF- *I look crazy or funny running?*

WHAT IF- *I run into someone that I don't want to see?*

WHAT IF- *I can't get someone to go with me on my walk or run for the day, "I don't want to do it alone"?*

WHAT IF- *I trip or fall and can't get back up again?*

WHAT IF- *I don't have a good pair of running shoes?*

Those are just a few questions that inhibit you from you getting off the treadmill and staying right where you are. Step outside of yourself and make it happen the possibilities could be endless. If you notice all of those questions start with a big **WHAT IF?** Maybe these questions could have some truth to them but just what if those questions didn't have a place in your life.

I will let you know that all of the What If's that pop in your head could also go like this with in your dream.

What if you run into someone that could help you achieve your goal?

What if you run but trip and someone is there to help you back up again?

What if someone could give you a pair of good shoes to run along the course of your journey?

What if you could take someone along with you and make you dream come to pass that much more quickly?

Now looking at all those (what if's) strike a very great concept. It makes you reconsider

DON'T CHASE YOUR
DREAMS CATCH THEM

your possibilities and takes the fear equation out of the picture. This makes one feel good and confident. Just maybe if you get off your treadmill that you are on right now those questions will be answered for you.

These questions don't strike with fear they strike with certainty. It is time you take a risk and live outside of your comfort zone. Don't live in the fear of the unknown anymore. This fear of the unknown should be the fear of never knowing if you could have done something to catch your dream. So I'm telling you not to live in it anymore.

The word fear truly means freeing your self. So when you think of fear think of being free. The acronym for fear is:

F-forget: Forgetting all of your failures and not holding onto those negative experiences.

E-eliminate: Eliminate all of the negative thoughts.

A-act: Acting on all your positive thoughts.

R-release: Releasing all of the forces, talents, and capabilities that help you move forward.

Understanding this as fear you will be able to make the jump from fear to freeing yourself from your mind.

For the fear acronym that shouldn't be thought of is this:

F-failure: Never making any attempts to realize your dreams.

DON'T CHASE YOUR DREAMS CATCH THEM

E-embarrassment: Being embarrassed means you're living for others thoughts and not your own.

A-abstain: Stopping once you have started on your way out the door.

R-routine: This means you stay on the treadmill and never get off and out of your comfort zone

Another two that most of you might be familiar with is these.

Face Everything and Run

Face Everything and Rise

The other one that international motivational speaker Tony Robbins uses is

"False Evidence Appearing Real."

If you live in fear using the positive acronym of it, then you will break free from the treadmill effect and won't be a prisoner to it.

I remember watching a movie one day entitled "UP IN TH AIR" starring George Clooney. He plays a character by the name of Ryan Bingham. There was a scene in the movie that stuck out to me. In that scene he was firing a man name Bob played by the actor; J.K. Simmons. The scene goes has follows.

Ryan Bingham: "Your children's admiration is important to you?"

Bob: "Yeah it was."

Ryan Bingham: "Well I'd doubt they ever admired you Bob."

Bob: "Hey Asshole aren't you supposed to be consoling me?"

Ryan Bingham: "I'm not a shrink Bob, I'm a wake up call."

Ryan Bingham: "You know why kids love athletes"?

Bob: "Because the screw lingerie models".

Ryan Bingham: "No that's why we love them".

Ryan Bingham: "Kids love athlete's because they follow their dreams".

Bob: "Well I can't dunk!"

Ryan Bingham: "No but you could cook."

Bob: "What are you talking about?"

Ryan Bingham: "Your resume say's you minored in French culinary arts, most students work at a fryer at KFC, but you bus tables at El Pekitor to support yourself, and then you get out of college and you come and work here."

Ryan Bingham: "How much did they first pay you to give up on your dreams?"

Bob: "twenty seven grand a year."

Ryan Bingham: "and when were you going to stop and come back to do what makes you happy?"

Bob: "Good Question."

*DON'T CHASE YOUR
DREAMS CATCH THEM*

Ryan Bingham: "I see guys who work for the same company their entire lives, guys exactly like you they clock in and clock out and they never have a moment of happiness."

Ryan Bingham: "You have an opportunity, here Bob, this is a rebirth, if not for you do it for your children."

At this point I noticed the light bulb go off in Bob's head from his expression on his face, after George Clooney's character says all of that to him.

Within this movie I wondered how many of you're at a job right now that as put you on the treadmill and kept you on it your whole time there?

You see there is a quote from Bruce Lee that I love and it helps you put into prospective on why you should get off the treadmill. His quote is this.

"Opportunity doesn't come to you, you have to go out and get it for yourself."

BRUCE LEE

Also in my younger brother's song **"WHAT ARE YOU WAITING FOR"** from the band; Marvlec talks about the same thing.

This song will be able to help you get off the treadmill and the effect won't last once you come to terms with these concepts that are in his lyrics. Trust me.

DON'T CHASE YOUR
DREAMS CATCH THEM

CHAPTER FIVE

DAYDREAM EFFECT

"All men dream, but not equally. Those who dream by night in the dusty recesses of their minds, wake in the day to find that it was vanity; but dreamers of the day are dangerous men, for they may act on their dreams with open eyes, to make them possible."

T.E. LAWERENCE

Now there is one other effect that will take place called the daydream

*DON'T CHASE YOUR
DREAMS CATCH THEM*

effect. We all have had this effect happen to us before. This effect happens strongly in your mind. Now with this effect it can happen at any moment and without notice. It usually happens when you are in a state of concentrated calmness.

I can remember for myself that I would usually have this happen to me in school. It is a state of trance that we go under within are own mind. I don't know if you can remember in grade school the teacher calling your name and you not responding. The non-response was due to this self-inducing trance that your daydream effect takes you on.

Other known as the:

Big Drift/Fog

All your senses such as auditory functions as well as your sight will be affected by this trance formation that you are under.

If you ever noticed for instance when you where talking to someone and they look as they're in a daze. Their eyes are glazed over; they look as if they're in a state of bewilderment and awe. You could wave your hand over their face and they won't blink and when you call out to them they don't respond even if you yell their name at the top of your lungs.

The reason for this the big drift/fog or self induce trance that I call the

*DON'T CHASE YOUR
DREAMS CATCH THEM*

daydream effect, is due to a number of reasons.

- Reason number one is that you don't share your dreams with anyone person you keep them to yourself.
- Reason number two is that you believe that your dreams are way to out there to be even spoken of.
- Reason number three is that you get lost in your own thoughts and stay within the confines of your daily activities, that you go on the big drift within your mind, this is for that reason of the glossy look that we have in our eyes when it happens to us.

Now this daydream effect unknown to our individual's self is dangerous to our dream and is affecting us from the catch. The only solution is to tell people about your dream no matter how out stretched you might think it is.

If you don't want to tell a number of people, I suggest that you at least tell one person within your life. Just in order to not get lost on the journey and your quest for that dream. You have to hold onto it with a firm grasp. It is like a cave diver, if the diver unhooks their line from your rope and starts wondering off in the dark cave without he or she knowing where their going, they will lose sight of the light very quickly and not be able to come back from it.

Like in sports such as football, baseball, and basketball if the players lose their grasp on the ball, then they just might have risked the victory for the big win for the game.

They only way around this *daydream effect* and from keeping them from affecting your dream is to get out of your own head. Throughout your life especially when you where a kid I'm sure you are aware of the phrase or been told the phrase (you have such a vivid imagination). Well it is this very power of this imagination that is carried over to your adulthood in the word we call dreams.

Your imagination is those dreams that we have. Without this so called vivid imagination that you have, it will be impossible for you to take action. I have no doubt you have also heard that from people throughout your life this phrase as well, that "you are such a day dreamer." Simply when people tell you that it's a clue to yourself, to start taking action.

Now by all means I'm not asking you to stop daydreaming and stop having an imagination. All I'm pointing out to you is that if you let the daydream effect take over your mind and stay in this effect, you won't be able to catch your dreams.

You will stay in the game of the chase and that is what you don't want to happen. How many of you have been in this daydream effect where that is all you do in life? If you can answer that question for yourself then you are on your way to having that dream in the palm of your hands.

DON'T CHASE YOUR
DREAMS CATCH THEM

Escape from your entrapment in your mind and let yourself be free. For you are the only one that can free your mind from the entrapment that is caused by this affect.

TEST TIME: *I want for you to answer a question the question is this:*

Q. What do you think is stronger **will power** *or* **imagination?**

I wondered how many of you said will power.

Now I want you close your eyes and will yourself not to imagine an elephant with a pink polka dot dress on, and drinking high tea with a queen.

*A.*_____

_____

I WOULD LIKE FOR YOU TO
FILL IN YOUR ANSWER.

Now within that question you found
the answer for yourself. Now you
understand the power of imagination and
just how important it is to the process of
you catching your dream. Imagination
brings forth transformation, which then
makes it into formation, then we get
realization and something tangible that
we ourselves can grasp on to. That is the
essence of power within your own
imagination.

That is why I'm not telling you to let
go of it all I'm saying is for to put you
hands out with the ability to step out side
of your normal boundaries within your
mind.

DON'T CHASE YOUR
DREAMS CATCH THEM

Just like **Morphes say's from the MATRIX**

MORPHES: "You got it let all go fear, doubt, and disbelief free your MIND!"

This is the answer for you to escape, from your own form of entrapment that you have placed yourself in. For you're the only one that will get in your head and stay there, if you let yourself be imprisoned to the *day dream effect*. Another words getting stuck in the analysis paralysis syndrome. Constantly analyzing so much that you get paralyzed from the over analyzing what could go wrong.

Don't question yourself within your quest for your dream. Just make those actions in your mind come alive by letting them see the outer world that you're creating.

So stop staring into space and start filling in that space. Once this happens the imprisonment will be no more and you will finally be free from the ***daydream effect!***

DON'T CHASE YOUR DREAMS CATCH THEM

CHAPTER SIX
BECOMING THE
CATCHER

How many of us have ever wanted to be catchers at some point in are lives. Well we are all catchers in our reality of our dreams. As long as we can see it, feel it, and believeth in it. Then your glove of hope can catch that dream. Being a catcher means more than just catching the ball it means going for the goal *(dream)!*

It's time for you to get up off the bench and start becoming the catcher of your game which is your *(dream)!* When you decide to make the decision to

DON'T CHASE YOUR
DREAMS CATCH THEM

become the catcher in your life you will notice a strange turn of events that take place.

First you have to become energized by your efforts to become a catcher. If you ever watch a football game or baseball game before, you surely don't see the man running down the field or in the in field all slow and sluggish to catch the ball. No you see the opposite you see him running with all his energy to catch the ball.

You have to be that ball of energy when it comes to you becoming the catcher of your dreams. You have to give more than your all. If you're not ready to do that then you will be watching your dream go by on the sidelines while you are sitting on the bench.

The most valuable player on football team is the receiver. You have to be the most valuable receiver on your team for your dreams. If a quarterback on a football team throws the football and the receiver isn't there to catch the ball then you really can't consider him a quarterback at all.

All he is; is a man throwing a ball in thin air. Without the receiver catching the football it's hard to make the touchdown. For the quarterback can't win the game without the receiver; being there to catch the ball and running down the field to make the touch down.

So becoming the catcher is what you want to do. You do this with one law and it is the only law you will have to follow in order to become the catcher of your dreams.

DON'T CHASE YOUR
DREAMS CATCH THEM

This law is called the ***LAW OF ACTION!!!*** I will go over this law of action and give you steps to take along your journey. With this law your chase is almost over believe it or not.

LAW OF ACTION

AND

HOW TO APPLY IT?

"Dreams pass into the reality of action. From the actions stems the dream again; and this interdependence produces the highest form of living".

Anais Nin

The law of action is the law that will help you within the chase of your dreams to become the catcher. If you

*DON'T CHASE YOUR
DREAMS CATCH THEM*

feel you're not making any movements, then you're not taking any actions. The law works like this. You have to make every move count towards your goal. The only way to do that is to have action behind every thought and have it being applied. People say that knowledge is power. In essence the source of any power in any knowledge is the ***application*** of knowledge being performed. Knowledge in itself holds no power.

So this is the only law that needs to be applied in action when catching your dream. If there is no action nothing will get done. You need to fill in the void through action. The void is the emptiness that is inside us all. We are born from the void. We live within the void until there is a tremendous amount of energy that fills that void with the resolution that we seek. Remember when I said something always comes out of nothing. That void of nothingness is the something that is missing from your life. This is what I'm talking about.

Well as of right now the void that is the missing is action. If there is no action it is difficult to get anything done. As of right now if I weren't doing the action of writing this book how would you be able to learn from this book? The simple answer is you wouldn't be able to learn from this book. Without my thoughts and the pure action of writing them down you wouldn't be reading this right now.

You see thoughts are the first element to the law of this action. It is the follow through after the initial thought

*DON'T CHASE YOUR
DREAMS CATCH THEM*

that fills in the void. So becoming the catcher to your dream is simple. Obey the *LAW of action* and follow through with your thoughts. If you don't get anything else from of this book, at least get this and please obey this one (LAW) and I assure you will become the catcher of your dreams.

My dad always tells me that the Jamaicans would say, "don't talk about it man, be about it." Which simply means walk the walk, do not; talk that talk because that won't get you anywhere. Everyone say's "talk is cheap" or "action speaks louder than words" and this is true. You can become a person that takes small actions or big ones; but I have to warn you of the big actions, they just might put you into a state of overwhelming feeling of hopelessness.

This feeling of hopelessness puts you into a state of non-movement. So I suggest you take small actions towards your goals. What this does, it gives you confidence to take on the bigger projects that are in your way to get to your desired results.

"Knowing is not enough we must apply" "Willing is not enough we must do."

BRUCE LEE

So the next chapter will help you with this hold that has you stagnant towards your dreams. I'm not telling you

*DON'T CHASE YOUR
DREAMS CATCH THEM*

to stop dreaming big. Yes please do dream big but the action to catch a big dream is better if they're smaller actions, which I call the catch of the day.

You've made the action to get this book and turn it page by page so within that action you're already taking the steps and obeying the law of action. I also want to take this time and tell anyone that is going to college or a trade school thanks. I have to give you kudos's for taking that very action step to get close to catching your dream.

So please keep going forward with the action and finish the book. Everything will make perfect sense at the end and you will become the catcher with the law of action. Without this law being followed your dream will never be caught and you will always stay in the game of the chase.

You have to put your efforts for your dream into motion.

The motions of action are the only way to combat this effect moving away from your mind and into the laws of action are crucial at this point in the chase.

CHAPTER SEVEN

CATCH OF THE DAY

"You must crawl before you stand, you must stand before your first step, only then will you be able to walk, in order to run towards your dreams."

Sean Alexander Hamilton

Now as I was already explaining to you in the last chapter. Taking small actions towards your dreams makes it easier to move toward your bigger goals.

DON'T CHASE YOUR DREAMS CATCH THEM

I simply made it into the catch of the day. If you take one action step a day towards your dream you're in the process of catching that dream and you're no longer within the chase. Everyday will be a catch of the day and you will end up that much more closer to fulfilling that dream. You should make it a set of steps to accomplishing your goals.

This will take a great amount of pressure off your mind and you won't be physically drained through out this process. No dream was caught over night by anyone. The fastest way to speed up any form of an evolving dream is to take it day by day.

If you noticed people that announced their dream to other people these dreams are usually hard to catch. They are most likely are not able to accomplish it and have trouble with catching anything within the realm of their dream.

The reason for this is we don't do anything but talk about it and I will tell you from personal experience you won't get anything done that way. So if you're talking and also applying the law of action you will feel and notice that you're on your way to making great things happen.

We tend to get lost in all of the tasks that would be necessary to catch that dream. That is when it is good to adapt this method so you don't get lost. The only solution and fix for this problem to all my soon to be catchers is to keep the catch of the day attitude.

*DON'T CHASE YOUR
DREAMS CATCH THEM*

If you stay in one spot for to long they say that you'll be in that spot without resolve. It is like for those people that decide to stay on the couch. Everyone has heard of the term couch potato. The objective is to keep moving forward with a single step one at a time.

If we have short-range goals we can make them come to the center of truth with a catch of the day. We take steps everyday and catch some part of our dream within this method. We have to have a catch everyday in order to be able to assist us in our chase for the dreams that lie ahead. You can use the model of someone that as been there before and this is called the mirror affect. You take what as been done before and you mirror it and make it your own.

We learn from our history. The history of the past tells us what to do, and what not to do. If you follow this simple task of action the compound of the law of action will take form like you wouldn't even believe. So make sure you have a catch of the day that counts towards your dream every single day.

That is the CATCH-22 to the catch of the day attitude. We all have a Catch-22 so go with it and stay on it. The **CATCH-22** is what will give you focus and power. It is the power of your own imagination that will come alive within your actions. So imagine your actions taking shape. Then watch the magic come alive.

DON'T CHASE YOUR
DREAMS CATCH THEM

CHAPTER EIGHT

DREAM CATCHER

*DON'T CHASE YOUR
DREAMS CATCH THEM*

"While he is dreaming he does not know it is a dream… only after he wakes does he know it was a dream. And someday there will be a great awakening when we know that this is all a great dream."

Zhuang Zhou Zi

(c. 369 BC-c. 286 BC)

Great Indian tribes from the past to present day would build these dream catchers and they would usually come from the elder shamans of the tribe. Now these mystical and almost magical totem's called dream catchers, was said to help the people in the tribe catch there bad dreams that we would refer to as nightmares.

Well this is exactly what you need to become. For you are the dream catcher by following these simple steps within this book you will have all the tools you need to become the dream catcher just like that from the Indian tribes.

Now in order to have this power that is within you, you will have to go under your own special rituals. Whether it is the power of visualization, meditation, cooperation, imagination, and

DON'T CHASE YOUR DREAMS CATCH THEM

understanding of specializations it will
be up to you.

By now you realize that you are your
own dream catcher. You hold in you the
vision, the mystery, the mystical, and the
magical power within you to become a
dream catcher. For you are your own
totem of self-assurance and fortitude to
be the dream catcher.

The power that lies within you is all
the power you will ever need. All you
have to do is find it in yourself. Most of
the time, this is the most difficult step in
the chase for your dream to find. A
power that is within you will shine
through like the radiate sun. Having to
find in your quest for your dream is the
ultimate power. Unfortunately this is
when it takes us through the most
difficult part within the chase.

YOU have to understand no one makes it to their dream unless they find their power and the sheer will to move toward that power. You are the only one that has this power. You have to be the ultimate elder shaman in your own tribe within your soul. Find the shaman within your spirit that is the spot you look in.

For the shamans hold onto the dream catchers. Once you become the dream catcher you can have any dream you want. Dream catchers aren't only successful people they can be anyone.

We look into are own life and we start to get discourage with it. It is because of this power that is within, that makes it all possible for anyone to catch his or her dreams. You have to hold onto your power and wield it with purpose. If you wake up with purpose you will be

DON'T CHASE YOUR
DREAMS CATCH THEM

able to see, believe, and achieve your dreams.

The desire to decide to wield this power comes down to a matter of choice. You can choose to settle without this inner strength of your inner dream catcher, or you can regret not even making the attempt to realize that dream and stay on chase for as long as you like.

But you have all the tools by now to become the dream catcher. All you have to do is make the power of choice come alive. With a final decision that's what it takes for the power within you to come alive. You have to see that within the tribe of your mind.

The reason this power works is the power of belief. Same thing goes for the actual tribes within the Indian tradition.

If the power of belief is not realized from the dream catchers that are given out to the tribe members then they won't work. Those individuals will still have the nightmares that haunt them in their sleep.

Your dream doesn't require the belief of someone else. The only belief that your dream requires is yours and that's it. If you believe in yourself and in your ability to make anything possible, then challenges that come your way will seem to be non-existent. So I want you to believe in your dream catcher abilities because your dream awaits you.

DON'T CHASE YOUR
DREAMS CATCH THEM

CHAPTER NINE

TIME'S A WASTEN

"I close my eyes, only for a moment and the moment's gone, all my dreams pass before my eyes a curiosity;

Dust in the wind. All they are is dust in the wind."

KANSAS

Your time is your most important element to the catch, we waste so much time within our day that we don't realize it until the day is over with. Every one of us has heard of the saying "you're not

DON'T CHASE YOUR DREAMS CATCH THEM

getting any younger." This is true for all of us. You don't have a lot of time on this earth so it is the most valuable asset that we have.

So wasting it is a big mistake. If you're not moving forward towards you greater calling, which is your dream than you're wasting your time along the way somewhere, that you're not aware of. It's your job to find out where and take account of this time and use it where it will be most useful.

There are a few master keys here that need to be followed so you don't waste any of your precious time.

MASTER KEYS TO FOLLOW!!!

- *MASTER KEY # 1.*
  Allotted Time:- you need
  to have your time allotted
  and divided up into
  sections to help you
  manage your time.
  Managed time is
  productive time.
- *MASTER KEY # 2.*
  Important Time:- you
  should find out what is
  the most important thing
  for you to concentrate
  on, in your quest for
  your dream. Please
  choose wisely this is a
  crucial key that will help

you to decide how to get there.

- *MASTER KEY # 3. Secured Time:- Secured time is time that you take just for yourself whether it is alone time, meditation time, or clarity time. This time helps you stay focused; it makes your mind clear from all the chaos that's in it. In order to be able to have time to help you stay managed.*

Now these keys are very important for you to be able to follow. With out these master keys all of your time will be wasted. We all want to be able to see our dreams realized. Now even if you pass on, and meet your creator that doesn't mean your dream won't be realized and caught.

Take for instant Martin Luther King Jr.'s Dream was realized through his sheer power of that envision that he saw every single day through the process of empowering that vision. He was able to empower that vision through his sound of pronouncing it over and over again.

Through his speech if you notice how many times he had said that he "I have a dream" you will feel and see the magic of pronouncing your thoughts. I will recite his entire speech on the next few pages. So you can understand what the power behind empowering your visions will do for you. I also suggest for anyone that hasn't seen this speech I

DON'T CHASE YOUR
DREAMS CATCH THEM

think you should find it on the Internet and watch it.

"I HAVE A DREAM"!!

Delivered 28 August 1963, at the Lincoln Memorial, Washington D.C.

By: Martin Luther King Jr.

I am happy to join with you today in what will go down in history as the greatest demonstration for freedom in the history of our nation.

Five score years ago, a great American, in whose symbolic shadow we stand today, signed the EMANCIPATION PROCLAMATION. This momentous decree came as a great beacon of light of hope to millions of

Negro slaves who had been seared in the flames of withering injustice. It came as a joyous daybreak to end the long night of their captivity.

But one hundred years later, the Negro still is not free. One hundred years later, the life of the Negro is still sadly crippled, by the manacles of segregation and the chains of discrimination. One hundred years later, the Negro lives on a lonely island of poverty in the midst of a vast ocean of material prosperity. One hundred years later, the Negro is still languished in the corners of American society and finds himself an exile in his own land. And so we've come here today to dramatize a shameful condition.

In a sense we've come to our nation's capital to cash a check. When the architects of our republic wrote the magnificent words of the Constitution and the Declaration of Independence, they were signing a promissory note to which every American was to fall heir. This note was a promise that all men, yes, black men as well as white men, would be guaranteed the " unalienable Rights" of "Life, Liberty and the pursuit of Happiness" It is obvious today that America has defaulted on this promissory note, insofar as her citizens of color are concerned. Instead of honoring this sacred obligation, America has given the Negro people a bad check; a check, which has come back, marked "insufficient funds." But we refuse to believe that the bank of justice is bankrupt. We refuse to believe that there are insufficient funds in the great vaults of opportunity of this nation. And so, we've come to cash this check, a check that will give us upon demand the riches of freedom and the security of justice.

We have also come to this hallowed spot to remind America of the fierce urgency of Now. This is no time to engage in the luxury of cooling off or to take the tranquilizing drug of gradualism. Now is the time to make real the promises of democracy. Now is the time to rise from the dark and desolate valley of segregation to the sunlit path of racial justice. Now is the time to lift our nation from the quicksand's of racial injustice to the solid rock of brotherhood. Now is the time to make justice a reality for all God's children.

DON'T CHASE YOUR
DREAMS CATCH THEM

It would be fatal for the nation to overlook the urgency of this moment. This sweltering summer of the Negro's legitimate discontent will not pass until there is an invigorating autumn of freedom and equality. Nineteen sixty-three is not an end, but a beginning. And those who hope that the Negro needed to blow off steam and will now be content will have a rude awakening if the nation returns to business as usual. And there will be neither rest nor tranquility in America until the Negro is granted his citizenship rights. The whirlwinds of revolt will continue to shake the foundations of our nation until the bright day of justice emerges.

But there is something that I must say to my people, who stand on the warm threshold, which leads into the palace of justice: In the process of gaining our rightful place, we must not be guilty of wrongful deeds. Let us not seek to satisfy our thirst for freedom by drinking from the cup of bitterness and hatred. We must forever conduct our struggle on the high plane of dignity and discipline. We must not allow our creative protest to degenerate into physical violence. Again and again, we must rise to the majestic heights of meeting physical force with soul force.

The marvelous new militancy which has engulfed the Negro community must not lead us to a distrust of all white people, for many of our white brothers, as evidenced by their presence here today, have come to realize that their destiny is tied up with our destiny. And they have come to realize that their

*DON'T CHASE YOUR
DREAMS CATCH THEM*

freedom is inextricably bound to our freedom.

We cannot walk alone.

And as we walk, we must pledge that we shall always march ahead.

We cannot turn back.

There are those who are asking the devotees of civil rights, "When will you be satisfied?" We can never be satisfied as long as the Negro is the victim of the unspeakable horrors of police brutality. We can never be satisfied as long as our bodies, heavy with the fatigue of travel, cannot gain lodging in the highways and the hotels of the cities. We cannot be satisfied as long as the negro's basic mobility is form a smaller ghetto to a larger one. We can never be satisfied as long as our children are stripped of their self-hood and robbed of their dignity by signs stating: "For Whites Only." We cannot be satisfied as long as a Negro in Mississippi cannot vote and a Negro in New York believes he has nothing for which to vote. No, no, we are not satisfied, and we will not be satisfied until "justice rolls down like waters, and righteousness like a mighty stream."

I am not unmindful that some of you have come here out of great trials and tribulations. Some of you have come fresh from narrow jail cells. And some of you have come from areas where your quest—quest for freedom left you battered by the storms of persecution and staggered by the winds of police brutality. You have been the

DON'T CHASE YOUR DREAMS CATCH THEM

veterans of creative suffering. Continue to work with the faith that unearned suffering is redemptive. Go back to Mississippi, go back to Alabama, go back to South Carolina, go back to Georgia, go back to Louisiana, go back to the slums and ghettos of our northern cities, knowing that somehow this situation can and will be changed.

Let us not wallow in the valley of despair, I say to you today, my friends.

And so even though we face the difficulties of today and tomorrow, I STILL HAVE A DREAM. IT IS A DREAM DEEPLY ROOTED IN THE AMERICAN DREAM.

I HAVE A DREAM that one day this nation will rise up and live out the true meaning of its creed: We hold these truths to be self-evident, that all men are created equal."

I HAVE A DREAM that one day on the red hills of Georgia, the sons of former slaves and the sons of former slave owners will be able to sit down together at the table of brotherhood.

I HAVE A DREAM that one day even the state of Mississippi, a state sweltering with the heat of injustice, sweltering with the heat of oppression, will be transformed into an oasis of freedom and justice.

I HAVE A DREAM that my four little children will one day live in the nation where they will not be judged by the color of their skin but the content of their character.

DON'T CHASE YOUR DREAMS CATCH THEM

I HAVE A DREAM TODAY!!

I HAVE A DREAM that one day, down in Alabama, with its vicious racists, with its governor having his lips dripping with the words of "interposition" and "nullification"—on e day right there in Alabama little black boys and black girls will be able to join hands with little white boys and white girls as sisters and brothers.

I HAVE A DREAM TODAY!!

I HAVE A DREAM that one day every valley shall be exalted, and every hill and mountain shall be made low, the rough places will be made plain, and the crooked places will be made straight; "and the glory of the Lord shall be revealed and all flesh shall see it together."

This is our hope, and this is the faith that I go back to the South with.

With this faith, we will be able to hew out of the mountain of despair a stone of hope. With this faith, we will be able to transform the jangling discords of our nation into a beautiful symphony of brotherhood. With this faith, we will be able to work together, to pray together, to struggle together, to go to jail together, to stand up for freedom together, knowing that we will be free one day.

And this will be the –this day will be the day when all of God's children will be able to sing with new meaning:

My country' tis of thee, sweet land of liberty, of thee I sing.

DON'T CHASE YOUR
DREAMS CATCH THEM

Land where my fathers died, land of the Pilgrim's pride,

From every mountainside, let freedom ring!

And if America is to be a great nation, this must become true.

And so let freedom ring from the prodigious hilltops of New Hampshire.

Let freedom ring from the mighty mountains of New York.

Let freedom ring from the heightening Alleghenies of Pennsylvania.

Let freedom ring from the snow-capped Rockies of Colorado.

Let freedom ring from the curvaceous slopes of California.

Let freedom ring from Stone Mountain of Georgia.

Let freedom ring from Lookout Mountain of Tennessee.

Let freedom ring from every hill and molehill of Mississippi.

From every mountainside, let freedom ring.

And when this happens, when we allow freedom ring, when we let it ring from every village and every hamlet, from every state and every city, we will be able to speed up that day when all of God's children, black men and white men, Jews, and Gentiles, Protestants and Catholics, will be able to join hands and sing in the words of the old Negro spiritual:

DON'T CHASE YOUR
DREAMS CATCH THEM

Free at Last!

Free at Last!

Thank God Almighty, we are free at last!!

It is within that speech is where we see as of today the affects of empowering the vision of your dream will do for you. Affirm that your dream is within your reach no matter what obstacle gets in your way.

I want all of the catchers out there to be able to fully realize your dream before it is to late. Even though your dream could be realized even in death, that is not my hopes for you. So have your actions be without delay. Use the reaction method.

The reaction method has to start out with action first then a reaction of momentum occurs within the initial action. If you keep going within your action then the reaction helps you stay on track, because you start to feel and see your efforts take form.

With each form that takes shape you will have a reaction into your next step. The span of events will take a chain of reaction steps once that action becomes your soul purpose for reaching that dream. Your dream will be realized and caught.

DON'T CHASE YOUR
DREAMS CATCH THEM

So don't let your actions be wasted. Time is something to be treasured whether it is your time with your loved one's, or time to find yourself.

For your time is undetermined so treasure it because you never know when that clock will stop. This time will seem to exist because you're no longer apart of that time continuum. People say that there is not enough time to do everything in one day.

The people that take their time and value it know of its importance. They're said to get the most out of their lives and have success in every aspect of it. Your time is the most valuable thing that we have on this planet, and you should make every second count.

Yesterday is history, tomorrow is a mystery, but today is a gift. That is why it is called the Present. So let go of the past, you're not going back that way. Don't worry about your future it will all play out if you're in the moment. But you must be present in that moment for it to workout the way you plan.

I once heard from one of my teachers Coach White was his name he told me.

"Fail to Plan, Plan to Fail."

So the time is NOW! To let go, move freely in the present time. That's when your life becomes important and you treasure it the most. No time like the present. So live for today it maybe your last.

DON'T CHASE YOUR
DREAMS CATCH THEM

"Dream as if you'll live forever, Live as if you'll die tomorrow."

James Dean

DON'T CHASE YOUR
DREAMS CATCH THEM

CHAPTER TEN

YOUR TIME IS NOW

Your time is now to achieve all that you can be and all that you ever wanted to become. Your time is now, not tomorrow, not in a week, not in a month, not in a year, your time is now. It's time to get out of your head and out into life. Your dreams are calling and reaching out to you.

Your time is now to live out your new years resolutions and achieve them. Don't wait another day to make something happen and get the ball rolling in order for you to catch it. Your time is now to catch it! So Catch It, Catch It, and Catch It. Please you owe it to yourself and anyone else that you've told your dream to. It's your soul purpose to make it happen for yourself.

I created a poster called Becoming A Dream Catcher before the re-release of this book. So I decided to put it in this book. Well the list that is, I suggest you get the poster for your room office or wherever you would like. So on the next few pages is that list.

DON'T CHASE YOUR
DREAMS CATCH THEM

BECOMING A DREAM CATCHER!

A. AIM WITH ACTION.

B. BELIEF IN BECOMING.

C. COURAGE TO CREATE.

D. DELIVER ON YOUR PROMISES TO YOURSELF.

E. EVOLVE YOUR DESTINY.

F. FORGE YOUR FUTURE.

G. GENERATE GROWTH.

H. HEAD TOWARDS YOUR DREAM.

I. IGNITE YOUR WAY.

J. JUST FOCUS.

K. KNOW YOU WILL HAVE IT.

L. LISTEN, LEARN, AND LEAD.

M. MAKE MOVES.

N. NEVER QUIT.

O. OPPORTUNITY EMBRACEMENT.

DON'T CHASE YOUR DREAMS CATCH THEM

P. PURSUE WITH PURPOSE.

Q. QUEST ATTAINMENT.

R. RELEASE DOUBTS.

S. SEEK NEEDED SKILLS.

T. TACKLE YOUR TIME.

U. UNLEASH YOURSELF TO THE WORLD.

V. VICTORY IN SIGHT.

W. WIN OVER YOUR EXCUSE.

X. XPECT TO INSPIRE.

Y. YOU GOT IT.

Z. ZOOM INTO YOUR
DREAMS!!!

*DON'T CHASE YOUR
DREAMS CATCH THEM*

So you see that is why your time is now to fulfill the gap within the void of your mind and bring light into the darkness of your DREAM. Only you can make the choice to do it right now. The longer you wait the harder it will become for you. Don't make the excuse that nothing can be done about it now because it has been to long already.

No more hesitating, no more waiting, and no more excuses. Your dream holds no prejudice, age, gender, color, physical capability, race, or time for that matter. Dreams are for everyone and anyone so there isn't a moment to lose. For Your Time Is Now and only Now!

Don't feel sorry for yourself anymore be empowered to know that you have everything you need right now.

Now you have the knowledge, all that you are lacking is the will.

Answer yourself these few questions but be honest with yourself.

Q. WHAT IS HOLDING YOU BACK?

A.

_____

_____

Q. WHAT WILL IT TAKE FOR YOU TO SEE YOUR MOMENT IS NOW?

*A.*_____

_____

Q. HOW LONG DOES YOUR DREAM NEED TO WAIT FOR YOU?

*A.*_____

_____

Q. SO WHAT ARE YOU WAITING FOR?

DON'T CHASE YOUR DREAMS CATCH THEM

*A.*_____

_____

Q. WHEN WILL YOU DECIDE FOR THE CHASE TO BE OVER?

A. RIGHT NOW!!

I ANSWERED THE LAST QUESTION FOR YOU BECAUSE I'M VERY PASSIONATE THAT YOUR TIME IS RIGHT NOW AND I FEEL NOTHING WILL STOP YOU.

"A ***Dream*** written down with a ***date*** becomes a ***goal***. A goal broken down into steps becomes a ***plan***. A plan backed by action becomes ***reality***."

Unknown

DON'T CHASE YOUR
DREAMS CATCH THEM

CHAPTER ELEVEN

THE GRAND TOUR

"Yesterdays Dreams Are Today's Reality."

Dan Pena

WELCOME: TO YOUR GRAND TOUR. NOW THAT YOU HAVE THE PURPOSE TO CATCH YOUR DREAM YOU'RE IN THE PROCESS OF CATCHING YOUR DREAM.

IT IS TIME TO SHOWCASE YOUR EFFORTS THROUGH YOUR GRAND TOUR. THE GRAND TOUR

DON'T CHASE YOUR DREAMS CATCH THEM

IS WHO YOU ARE BECOMING IN
THE PROCESS OF THE CHASE.

WHEN YOU LOOK INTO THE
WINDOW GLASS OF YOUR
GRAND TOUR YOU SHOULD SEE
NOTHING BUT POSSIBILITES,
GREAT ACCOMPLISHMENTS,
AND ACHIEVEMENTS THAT
COULD ONLY BE CAUGHT BY
YOU!

THE GRAND TOUR OF YOUR
DREAM WILL INSPIRE YOU TO
CATCH ALL THE OTHER
DREAMS THAT YOU EVER
WANTED IN YOUR LIFE. IT WILL
GIVE YOU THE CONFIDENCE TO
BREAKDOWN ALL OF THE
WALLS AND BARRIERS THAT
ONLY YOU HAVE PUT UP FOR
YOURSELF.

YOUR GRAND TOUR WILL BRING YOU CLOSER TO ANY ACHIEVEMENT THAN YOU EVER THOUGHT POSSIBLE. IT WILL SHOW CASE AND WILL PUT YOU ON DISPLAY FOR THE WHOLE WORLD TO WATCH IN AMAZEMENT AS YOU ACHIEVE YOUR DREAM.

THE GRAND TOUR IS THE REALITY OF YOUR DREAM. IT IS THE WAKING DREAM, LIVING DREAM, BREATHEING DREAM, WALKING DREAM AND YOUR'E ACTUAL DREAM. NOTHING IN THIS MOMENT OR IN ANY FUTURE MOMENTS WILL STOP YOU FROM THIS POINT.

YOUR GRAND TOUR IS YOUR ENLIGHTMENT SHINING

DON'T CHASE YOUR DREAMS CATCH THEM

THROUGH THE HEAVENS DOWN
ON EARTH AND IT IS THE
CREATOR TELLING YOU A JOB
WELL DONE MY LOYAL
SERVANT.

YOUR CREATOR WILL SAY,
"YOU'VE SET OUT WHAT WAS
MEANT OF YOU. WHAT WAS
MEANT OF YOU WAS FOR YOU
TO FULFILL THAT GREAT
ACCOMPLISHMENT WHICH YOU
HAVE AND THANK YOU."

THIS IS WHAT THE GRAND
TOUR IS AND FEELS LIKE. YOU
WILL BE THE ONLY ONE THAT
WILL BE ABLE TO FEEL THIS
FEELING. WHEN YOU FINALLY
STEP INTO YOUR DREAM
INSTEAD OF RUNNING FROM IT.

SO FROM THIS MOMENT ON
THERE WILL BE NO MORE
RUNNING AND NO MORE
CHASING ONLY YOUR HANDS
HELD UP HIGH SO YOU CAN
FINALLY SAY TO YOURSELF
AND THE WORLD " I HAVE
FINALLY CAUGHT MY DREAM".
"NOW WHAT ABOUT YOU?"

YOU'RE UP AND IT IS YOUR
TURN. I'M PASSING ON THE
GLOVE TO YOU SO YOU CAN
MAKE YOUR LAST RUN AND
CATCH YOUR DREAM.

SO GOOD LUCK IN YOUR
QUEST FOR THE CATCH!!!

YOU KNOW HOW THEY SAY;
"DREAMS DO COME TRUE."

DON'T CHASE YOUR
DREAMS CATCH THEM

**THEY ONLY COME TRUE IF YOU
GO TO THEM AND CATCH THEM!**

**I WISH YOU WELL AND MUCH
SUCCESS!!!**

**REMEMBER YOUR DREAM
AWAITS YOU. SO GO CATCH IT!!!**

DON'T CHASE YOUR
DREAMS CATCH THEM

ACKNOWLEDGEMENTS

I want to acknowledge the two people in my life that never let anything get in their way when going after their dreams, my mother Vicki Lynn Hamilton who in every aspect of her life she always went after everything that she wanted and didn't let anything stand in her way. She will always be my guiding light from heaven as she watches me from above. I also want to thank my dad William Thomas Hamilton for always telling me to reach for the stars and never to stop reaching.

DON'T CHASE YOUR
DREAMS CATCH THEM

ALSO WRITTEN BY

SEAN ALEXANDER HAMILTON

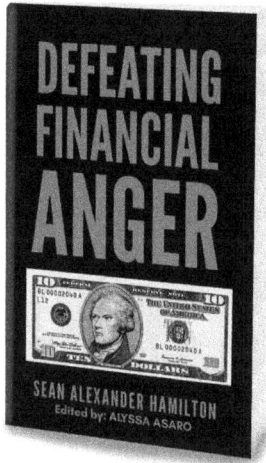

DON'T CHASE YOUR
DREAMS CATCH THEM

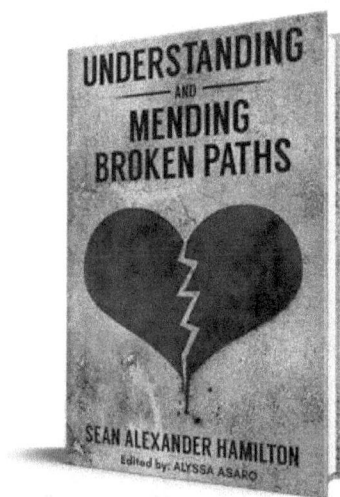

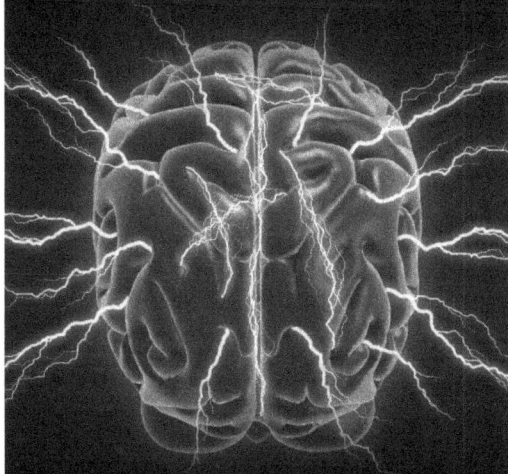

SPECIAL REPORT:
DMT SYSTEM

DISCIPLINE MIND TRACK SYSTEM
(DMTS)

"Remember your dreams are real,
all you have to do is wake up to make
them a reality."

Sean Alexander Hamilton

Thanks for Reading

ALEXANDER HAMILTON'S
INSIGHTS

*DON'T CHASE YOUR
DREAMS CATCH THEM*

DON'T CHASE YOUR
DREAMS CATCH THEM

*DON'T CHASE YOUR
DREAMS CATCH THEM*

www.ingramcontent.com/pod-product-compliance
Lightning Source LLC
Chambersburg PA
CBHW060022100426
42740CB00010B/1562